£1·50

KV-372-932

Ki.61-I-Kai, 244th Air Combat Regiment, 2nd Company, Home Island Defence. Standard green camouflage on natural metal, red stripe under cockpit with five white "kill" marks, red fuselage band and tail; white fuselage lightning stripe. Yellow leading edge, brown spinner, indigo anti-glare panel.

KAWASAKI Ki.61/Ki.100 HIEN
IN JAPANESE ARMY AIR FORCE SERVICE

**Compiled and written by
Richard M. Bueschel**

**Illustrated by
Richard Ward**

ACKNOWLEDGEMENTS

Unique amongst Japanese fighters of the Second World War period in that it was the only type with an inline engine, albeit a not very successful power unit, the Ki.61 was one of the most colourful of JAAF types especially within the Home Defence squadrons. Thanks are due to all who assisted with material and information whose names are listed below in alphabetical order:
Acme, Hideya Ando, Hal Andrews, Koku Asahi, Asahigraph, Peter M. Bowers, R. Bueschel, J. Canary, E. Deigan, F. C. Dickey Jr., Akira Hasegawa, Kuku Jidai, Kawasaki, Koku-Fan, Sekei no Kokuki, W. T. Larkins, Maru, R. C. Mikesh, M. Olmstead, M. B. Passingham, N. Saito, Al Schmidt, Warren Shipp, Hiko Shonen, Seiso Tachibana, M. Toda, USAF, US Army, USN, USSBS.

Ki.61-I-Kai, Chinese Nationalist Air Force, Nanyuan airfield, Peiping, China, September 1945. Dark green uppers, pale grey unders brown spinner, natural metal rudder with green dapple, red fuselage stripe.

Published by: Osprey Publications Limited, England

Editorial Office: P.O. Box 5, Canterbury, Kent, England

Subscription & Business Office: P.O. Box 25, 707 Oxford Road, Reading, Berkshire, England

The Berkshire Printing Co. Ltd. © Osprey Publications Ltd. SBN 85045 026 8 1971 Not for sale in U.S.A.

JAAF pilots regarded Ki.100-1b as an even match for the P-51D, and superior to F6F Hellcat (N. Saito via Bueschel)

Kawasaki Hien Model 1a of the 78th Air Combat Regiment at the "Southern Front" in the jungles of New Guinea (N. Saito via Bueschel).

KAWASAKI Ki.61/Ki.100 HIEN

For Lieutenant Minoru Shirota the year of decision dawned on Japan with extended rays of despair. One year ago the war front was thousands of miles away in thought and measure, with the fighting in New Guinea. But now, a short year later, the front was only thousands of feet away—straight *up*—as giant B-29 bombers took the measure of Japan. On 4 January 1945, Shirota finished his last words on paper, ran to his beloved Hien fighter when the alarm sounded to announce the imminent arrival of B-29's over Nagoya, climbed high for about six minutes, sighted his foe, and dived!

The excitement of being an Army pilot, the joy of flight, and the pride of nationalism all showed up in Minoru Shirota's writing. Both pilot and author, he turned his creative talents to the pen and earned a large and enthusiastic audience throughout wartime Japan. Shirota thought of his Kawasaki Type 3 Fighter as his mount, combat as a chivalrous joust, pilots of his regiment as fellow knights of the Round Table, the air above as his life-giving environment, and the treasured islands of homeland Japan as his Camelot. Through his many printed articles in newspapers and magazines Shirota became an unofficial spokesman for the Japanese Army Air Force, and a hero to impressionable Japanese youth. His readers followed his every word, and deed.

As the 3-ton Hien approached the 67-ton B-29 at increasing speed the inhuman aiming of automatic turrets zeroed-in on the small Japanese fighter. They didn't stop it. Moments later the pencil-nosed humanly-guided missile smacked into the B-29's fuselage right behind the wing in a perfect Special Attack hit. As Lieutenant Shirota's life burst the bomber's engines began to tear the giant apart. Down below, on a roof top, one of Shirota's friends of the press filmed the whole spectacle. It made the morning headlines. The aviation writer became a martyr, and began a blood bath of patriotism in the airspace over Japan.

The aircraft that carried Shirota to his youthful death, and the one most widely used for air-to-air *Taiatari* "body crashing" attacks, was the Kawasaki Ki.61 Type 3 Fighter Hien, translated as "Flying Swallow". The first single-seat fighter to enter Japanese Army Air Force service after the Pacific War began, the Hien was unique as the only inline-engine fighter to be used by Japan in combat in the war years. It started its mechanical life as an arrogant Japanese attempt to improve on the German Messerschmitt Bf.109 E/2 Fighter and ended it as a supercharged radial-engined interceptor that looked so much like other Japanese fighters it was never recognized by its opponents as a distinct aircraft type.

Help from Europe

The Ki.61 series could be described as Kawasaki's ultimate product. While other Kawasaki aircraft were used by the J.A.A.F., with many experimental types in process at the war's end, no other Kawasaki type was produced so long, in such numbers or in such model profusion. The Hien was a monument to Kawasaki's faith in the inline-engine fighter, and the instrument that ultimately revealed the clay feet of this technical *tour de force*. It was the year that Kawasaki lost out in the Army Type 97 Fighter competition when company representative Sei Yamasaki, in Germany under the orders of managing director Masayuki Nemoto, began an aggressive pursuit of the manufacturing rights for the new Daimler-Benz DB.601A engine. Kawasaki had achieved a measure of success with its 92-Sen and Ki.10 95-Sen series of inline-powered biplane J.A.A.F. fighters, but lost its position as the leading Army fighter producer in 1937 when its Ki.28 experimental fighter was passed over in favour of the radial-powered Nakajima Ki.27. This procurement defeat promised to stunt the growth of the maverick Army aircraft producer, and all stops were pulled to regain the technological advantage over the domestic aircraft producing competition.

The long-standing Kawasaki engineering alliance with German interests offered a way out of the dilemma. Through friendship, persuasion, the contacts of Dr Vogt, former Kawasaki Chief Designer then working with Blohm und Voss in Hamburg, and with hard currency, a licence agreement between the German engine producer and the hopeful Japanese fighter manufacturer was carved out late in 1939. Kawasaki now had complete rights to the most powerful new inline engine in the world, and a chance to recapture the attention of the Japanese Army. With Hisashi Tojo, brother of wartime premier Hideki Tojo, on the Kawasaki board of directors the new acquisition quickly received recognition in high places. In February 1940 the Army gave Kawasaki developmental contracts for the Ki.60 Heavy and Ki.61 Light Fighters utilizing the German power plant and its Japanese adaptions. By April, Kawasaki was actively promoting its gain and illustrating a modern low wing inline-engine fighter in its advertising before Chief Designer, Takeo Doi, even had the first of the two new projects completed on paper. With the Ki.60 Doi and his co-designer Skni Owada, armed with the same power plant, set out to out-design the Messerschmitt Bf.109 then under development in Germany. Three DB.601A engines imported from Germany in April 1940 as patterns for Kawasaki development were assigned to the Ki.60 project, and by March 1941 the first prototype was ready for flight as the Ki.6001. The aircraft was so small and heavy it terrified its Army sponsors. The second prototype, finished in summer 1941, had a larger wing to take the power and a redesigned cowling for better cooling and lines. Two of the four machine guns of the first prototype were dropped, with German Mauser MG-151 20 mm. cannon mounted in the new wings of the Ki.6002. The top speed checked out at 348 m.p.h., a disappointment as designers Doi and Owada had hoped for about 375 m.p.h. The cannon armament was dropped (the basic engineering work would reappear later in a series of Hien modifications) and the cowl area further refined in the Ki.6003. Armament was changed to four 12.7 mm. machine guns and the top speed jumped to 354 m.p.h. But it still wasn't enough to counteract the genuine pilot fear of such a heavy hit-and-run fighter. Even before Messerschmitt Chief Test Pilot Willi Stör's Me.109 E/2 fighters arrived in Japan in June 1942 for evaluation, the fate of the Ki.60 had been clearly decided. The aircraft was too dangerous for J.A.A.F. consideration, and in December 1940 the companion Ki.61 Light Fighter project earned priority consideration as the Ki.60 work was shelved.

Where the Ki.60 had been positioned as an interceptor, the Ki.61 was developed as a Light Fighter in the Ki.43 Type 1 Fighter Hayabusa class, although heavier and faster than the Nakajima product it was designed to replace. The Kawasaki firm had the field to itself as the Ki.61 project was assigned to the company on a non-competitive basis, a procedure that had started with the Ki.43. A back-up project was assigned to Nakajima as the Ki.62 to utilize the Kawasaki adaptation of the German inline engine, but it was never considered as a threat to the success and Army acceptance of the Ki.61 Fighter and was later dropped. By July 1941 the Kawasaki re-design of the Daimler-Benz DB.601A in working shape as the Kawasaki Ha.40, with prototypes of the power plant made available to the Kawasaki experimental shops for mounting in Ki.61 airframes. Prototype Ki.6101 was finished off at the Gifu plant in December 1941, a matter of days after Japan had committed herself to war at Pearl Harbour.

Although bigger and heavier than the earlier Ki.60 series while utilizing the same basic power plant, the Ki.6101 was considerably faster. Designers Doi and Owada were the praise receivers when the prototypes reached a top speed of 367 m.p.h. in tests at Kagamigahara airfield early in 1942. Hand-made prototypes were put together two or three at a time to create a total of twelve Ki.61 Army Experimental Fighter prototypes during the first six months of 1942. Each new test model differed in details as various cowls, cockpit covers, controls and armament variations were tried. But even before the flight evaluation trials were conducted the Army authorized Kawasaki to commit to a production line and buy the necessary tooling and raw materials. Takeo Doi's design was literally bought off the drawing board as the clouds of war moved across Pacific skies. By August 1942 test models were being built with the production tooling to iron out the kinks in the manufacturing line.

Problems and Production

The Army's enthusiasm for the new fighter started on a high, but was soon brought down to earth in a series of unexplained accidents that destroyed some of the Ki.61 prototypes and cost the lives of a number of test pilots known for their experience and skill. Any new machine has problems, and a device as complicated as an aircraft will always have parts that don't fit or components that won't work. The Ki.61 series of prototypes were no exception, and the fact that a complicated hydraulic system, self-sealing gas tanks, armoured pilot protection and other modern-for-its-day devices were fitted to an Army fighter for the first time added to the confusion. But the problems were greater than that, for they remained unanswered. Flying prototype Ki.6104 in late spring 1942 a Kawasaki pilot crashed into the top of a mountain while flying from the testing field at Kagamiga-

hara to Tachikawa. The accident was chalked up to an error in navigation, until later in the summer when another prototype blew up in the air, killing Kawasaki Chief Test Pilot Kataoka. The problems with what was revealing itself to be a touchy engine in the Ha.40, and the many new features of the airframe, led to a fear that the Ki.61 might be jinxed. But other returns were more rewarding, for the testing results proved the Army's new fighter to be a better performer than the Ki.43 Model II Hayabusa prototype, a captured American Curtiss P-40E, or even the vaunted Messerschmitt Bf.109 E/2 based on comparison flights on all of these aircraft at Kagamigahara in 1942. By August the fighter had all but official Army acceptance and production got under way with confirmation the following year as the Type 3 Fighter Hien.

Coming of Age in Combat

The Hiens' first taste of combat was prophetic, for it took place over Japan. While flying an early Ki.61 prototype from the training field at Mito, on 18 April 1942, Army Lieutenant Umekawa ran into Doolittle's Tokyo raiders in the first American bombing attack on Japan. Umekawa turned to pursue one of the North American B-25 Mitchell bombers skimming across Japan at treetop heights, but had to break off quickly due to low fuel and the erratic behaviour of his machine guns. One of the American raiders, Captain Charles R. Greening of Hoquiam, Washington, spotted the skinny fighter over Japan and reported its presence to the U.S.A.A.F. after his return to safety. This sighting was misinterpreted as it was believed to indicate that Japan was importing or producing Messerschmitts which were then expected in the other Pacific war theatres.

This chance meeting north of Tokyo was only a prelude to the actual commitment to combat of the Hien. It would be a year before the Ki.61 met American aircraft in the air again. Great changes would occur in that year, and the Hien would become one of the J.A.A.F's last hopes to counteract that change.

When an army is winning its battles not many questions are asked. But when it starts to lose, panic often sets in. Few military establishments in the world have ever been able to resist the temptation to over-react to a problem situation. The combat use of the Hien became a classic example of this universal military syndrome. Untried and not yet ready for overseas combat, the positive values of the Hien were literally thrown away on a long-shot gamble in the jungles of New Guinea. The whole operation was a fiasco, and it cost the J.A.A.F. dearly. In retrospect it cost them the air war. When the Japanese advance reached its limit in the Southwest Pacific in the autumn of 1942 following the American invasion of Guadalcanal, it was obvious that the Imperial Japanese Navy couldn't handle the job of holding the line alone. In August 1942, the very month that American Marines landed in the Solomons, the J.A.A.F. received its first production Hien. By the end of the year thirty-four had been built as the Ki.61-Ia, and by March of 1943 the J.A.A.F. had received over a hundred. It was decided to throw the new fighter into action on the "Southern Front", and an immediate crash programme of unit formation and training was started to get the Hien into action as soon as possible. Examples of the Ki.61-Ia were rushed to the Army Aviation Maintenance School at Tokorozawa early in 1943, followed by the conversion of the 68th Fighter Regiment to the new fighter in March and the 78th Fighter Regiment in April. The pilots of both units soon found themselves at the Akeno Army Flying School to receive pre-flight and flight training on the heaviest fighter yet to enter Japanese Army service.

While the training progressed, plans were made to strengthen Japan's positions on the "Southern Front" during a combat lull lasting almost six months. This was a far cry from the rapid Japanese victories of 1942, but the forces of Japan needed time to collect their wits and firm up their holdings to prepare for the coming Allied reaction. An Army aircraft exodus to Rabaul was begun, and starting in April 1943 the Hien entered the stream as the 68th and 78th Regiments moved overseas. The 4th

Air Army was being formed in New Britain for defence of the Solomons and later eventual placement on New Guinea in a logistics exercise that continually strained the J.A.A.F's capacity to keep up with the demand. In an island-hopping supply route that over-tested the ability of Army pilots to navigate over open water to their new bases in the Southwest Pacific, the Hien struggled its way to war.

The original plan was to have an equal force of Army and Navy aircraft in the Solomons area to defend the threatened Japanese bases. From the very beginning the Army could not live up to its commitment. The required number of aircraft were assembled in Japan and the Empire, but the delivery losses mounted so rapidly that the idea was soon abandoned. The Hien fighters of the 78th Regiment coming from Japan were taken on carriers in late April to the major Japanese Pacific base at Truk, and from there flown to Rabaul. Inexperience, engine unreliability, and poor radio and navigation equipment cost the new units dearly. In the first delivery flight of thirty fighters the unit got off course, losing eighteen of the aircraft in forced landings on a reef, although most of the pilots were saved. Design "bugs", still uncorrected in the new Hiens rushed into service, also caused problems. In one horrible delivery, flight mechanical malfunction of a Ki.61-Ia fuel-valve leading from the range-extending wing-mounted drop tanks led to the ditching of most of the fighters in the water between Truk and Rabaul. The lucky pilots who remained in the air watched helplessly as their friends hung on to their floating fighters, finally sinking into the shark-infested sea.

The 68th Regiment, moving south in May, made the trip entirely by air flying from the Ryukyu Islands to Formosa, then the Philippines and across the northern edge of New Guinea to Rabaul. By the end of May, after the hazardous flights, both regiments barely had thirty Hien fighters each at Rabaul and had already lost a number of their skilled pilots. The build-up continued, however, as the 4th Air Army filled the Rabaul airfields at Vunakanau, Lakunai and Rapopo with over 300 aircraft by the middle of June. Later other units would move to the "Southern Front", including the 33rd Hien Fighter Regiment, as the J.A.A.F. stripped Indo-China, Malaya, Burma, China and Manchoukuo of pilots and units to defend the southern borders of Japan's new empire.

One of the first jobs assigned to the Hien units of the 4th Air Army at Rabaul was the protection of supply convoys to New Britain, New Ireland, and the expanding bases in New Guinea. As their forces grew, some of the Army aircraft even took part in raids on the Solomons. But the future home of the growing J.A.A.F. forces was New Guinea, with all but the southern shoreline largely under Japanese control. In an agreement worked out at Imperial Headquarters in Tokyo, plans were made to leave the Solomon area, with defence originating from Rabaul, in Navy hands while assigning the Army the responsibility of New Guinea to protect the Japanese ground forces there and blunt any Allied offensive. The Army, long pre-conditioned to fighting the Soviet Union on the Asiatic mainland, now found itself in charge of a single island continent.

It was on Vunakanau airfield at Rabaul that the Ki.61-Ia was first clearly confirmed by American reconnaissance planes as a distinct Japanese type. Much has been said about the assignment of the Allied code name "Tony" to the Hien during this period because it was originally thought to be an Italian design. The truth of the matter is that "Tony" looked so different from other Japanese fighters it was assigned a unique name to quickly separate it in combat reports. The "Italian Fighter" story was merely a logical excuse for the name. In early reports the code name "Mike" was used, this at a time when the thin-nosed fighter was believed to be a Messerschmitt, but this was soon clarified during the Hien's short stay at Rabaul.

Defeat in New Guinea

The establishment of the J.A.A.F. in New Guinea began

to take positive shape in June 1943. The headquarters units stationed at Ambon and the combat units at Rabaul were held in readiness to move as soon as the Army engineering units had prepared their bases on the northern and northeast coast of New Guinea. The 4th Air Army found itself responsible for New Guinea east of longitude 140° stretching from major fields at Wewak, Dagua, But, Aitape and Tami all the way back along the New Guinea coast to Hollandia, Nubia and Manua. Forward fields suitable for Hien use were set up at Madang, Alexishafen, Lae, Salamana, Finschhafen and Saidor. With some 324 planes in the 6th Air Division and an additional 156 planes in the 7th Division plus eighty-four more at Ambon, the units of the 4th Air Army crossed over from Rabaul and Ambon in July and August, setting up their new headquarters at Wewak. By 20 September the shift had been completed and the J.A.A.F. was out of New Britain in force.

The move to New Guinea was barely under way when the J.A.A.F. installations came under constant attack by the American 5th Air Force, also stationed on New Guinea to the far south. For the first time in the Pacific War both sides were firmly established on the same land mass separated only by a mountain range in the middle. The result was a direct and constant confrontation of forces. Also, for the first time, the Japanese were on the defensive and were fighting a different kind of war. The Ki.61-Ia Hien fighters, now being joined by the 4 × 12.7 mm. machine gun Ki.61-Ib model, had too much to do. While the Nakajima Ki.43 Hayabusa was on hand at New Guinea in force, it was the Hien that pulled much of the convoy protection duty covering the movement of goods from Rabaul to Wewak, in addition to the airfield defence duties which required rapid interception of raiding Allied aircraft. This was almost an impossible task, for the Japanese did not have radar and more often than not were caught with their aircraft on the ground. As the bombers and fighters of the American 5th Air Force slashed into their fields after dropping down to the shoreline following a flight over the Owen Stanley mountain range, the J.A.A.F. units only had moments to get ready to defend themselves.

The first hammer-like blow came the night of 17 August 1943. Allied reconnaissance had been watching the build-up at Wewak and the surrounding airfields since May. Then, when the fields were packed with aircraft, including over 200 fighters, the American 5th Air Force struck in an attempt to pin down the J.A.A.F. while Allied forces invaded Lae and Salamana. Striking at the four 4th Air Army airfields at Wewak, But, Dagua and Boram, American heavy and medium bombers escorted by seventy-four P-38 Lightning fighters caught the Japanese on the ground. The next morning they hit the fields again and kept it up. At the end of five days the 4th Air Army was a shambles with an estimated 250 aircraft lost in the air and on the ground, with most lost to bombing and strafing. The strikes were so rapid; the Allied pilots often caught the Japanese in the open with their engines turning over ready to take off. Even when the defending Hien pilots got into the air they were outclassed. In the 18 August morning attack alone the J.A.A.F. lost twenty-eight out of thirty fighters in the air while the Americans lost three. The losses were not always so one-sided, as almost a dozen Hien "aces" came out of the frantic air fighting during the next year. Most of them died there, although some survived to fight in their Kawasaki fighters later in the Philippines and over Japan.

The fast-hitting Allied air forces were not the only problems facing the Hien units in New Guinea. There were other, slower and equally damaging forces at work to cut down and help destroy the beleagured Hiens and J.A.A.F. personnel. The hot, sticky climate was a health hazard to man and machine. Like the engine of a finely tuned sports car, the Ha.40 power plant of the Ki.61 couldn't be left running on the ground too long, or it would quickly overheat and cause main bearing problems. The ever-present dust at Wewak was sucked into the air intakes past inadequate filters, leading to engine breakdowns. Natural filters, such as sponge gourds, were

Kawasaki Ha.40 engine prototypes were not available for the Ki.60, so imported Daimler-Benz DB.601A power plants were used (Hideya Ando via Bueschel).

shipped out from Japan and jammed into the intakes to protect the delicate cylinder walls. Disease also took its toll, with many Japanese in the tropics for the first time in their lives. Malaria, fungus and general jungle rot kept many incapacitated, while the equally-suffering Allied air forces hit the Japanese bases again and again. Sickness kept Hien pilots out of the air, thereby further reducing the number of fighters that could be placed over the airfields during an attack.

While this unchecked loss of equipment droned on endlessly in New Guinea, the replacement of new aircraft slowed to a crawl. It wasn't until November 1943 that Hien production went over 100 aircraft a month, and then plateaued at around 150 per month thereafter with but few exceptions. The fighters that were produced were beset with problems, further aggravated by haphazard factory inspection of the finished product before delivery. A substantial number of the hundreds of Hien fighters that finally reached New Guinea couldn't be used when they arrived. Part of the Kawasaki manufacturing line was then turned over to spare parts production to keep the Hiens already produced in the air, further slowing the production rate.

Maintenance in the field made the situation more difficult. Only a handful of really good Hien mechanics were ever trained, with most of the ground crews inexperienced in maintenance fundamentals, much less in the sophisticated complexities of the Hien. From the very beginning the inline-engine cooling and hydraulic systems leaked. It was as if Japanese designers couldn't keep liquids under control in an aircraft. Starting with built-in leaks, and faced with further combat damage, the ground crews almost gave up. Perfectly good Hien fighters in all other respects were inoperable and were stored in the jungles around New Guinea airfields. Useless on the ground, and soon spotted by raiding Allied attackers, they were shot

The Ki.60 differed externally from the parallel Ki.61 in having a snub nose, short moment-arm and shorter wings (M. Toda via Bueschel).

up and destroyed by the score. Spare parts were also in short supply, or didn't exist at all. Convoy after convoy carrying "Tony" fighter spares among their cargo were sunk or diverted. New Guinea was virtually cut off. Major repairs were practically impossible. Ha.40 engine breakdowns, which were frequent, required heavy repair equipment which never arrived. The closest Ki.61 repair depot was at Halmahera, over a thousand miles away from Wewak, and when a Hien required an engine change it had to be shipped all the way back to Manila in the Philippines. Attempts were made to supply spare Hien parts from Japan, but even this was of little help as many of the parts were in short supply or just not available.

In spite of its many problems the Hien was well liked by its pilots, and generally preferred over its Ki.43 Hayabusa sister fighter. All models of the Ki.61, from start to finish, handled easily. A little clumsy in a dog fight by the standards of the other nimble Japanese Army fighters built by Nakajima, the Hien was still more manoeuvrable than the Allied fighters it opposed until the arrival of the F6F Hellcat and P-51 Mustang. The Hien fuselage was sturdy and could take a greater beating in combat than any of the earlier Japanese radial engine fighters.

"Tony" quickly became the most feared Japanese fighter in the New Guinea skies, with the Ki.61 fighters that got into the air scoring comparatively well against the P-40, P-39 and P-38 fighters flown by the American and Commonwealth air forces. When in trouble, a Hien pilot could dive out of it very quickly with assurance that the aircraft would hold together. Safely protected with armour for pilot and fuel, at least to some degree, Hien pilots tended to be more aggressive than Army pilots flying the lighter Ki.43 Hayabusa. From the very beginning in New Guinea, when "Tony" fighters were flying out of the Madang-Alexishafen area to protect the construction of their new facilities at Wewak, the pilots of the new fighters were determined and ready to fight. As the losses mounted, new pilots and fighters were pushed into Wewak to keep defensive strength up. Hollandia was built up as a supply base, with new Hien fighters arriving there from Japan moved eastward to Wewak.

By the latter part of 1943 the J.A.A.F. was in obvious retreat. Following the disastrous losses in the Wewak area, on 15 March 1944 the 4th Air Army evacuated its positions and moved its headquarters all the way west to Hollandia. But the fiasco of New Guinea had gone too far. By the middle of April the Allies were ready to invade Hollandia itself. Once again the J.A.A.F. was caught on the ground, and by 15 April it was estimated that 340 aircraft had been destroyed at Hollandia. Saving what little it could after further losses, the shattered 4th Air Army again pulled out and set itself up at Menado in the Celebes. The air over New Guinea was finally owned by the Allies and the ring closed.

It wasn't until the end of 1943 that the first Hien was captured intact by the Allies, giving the Americans a close look at the respected Japanese fighter. Late in December American forces landed at Cape Gloucester in order to isolate Rabaul and cut the supply lines to New Guinea. On 30 December the Cape Gloucester airfield was taken by American Marines. Hidden under the brush in almost perfect condition was a Hien of the J.A.A.F. 68th Fighter Regiment that had been used on daylight convoy patrol. Quickly spirited out of the area for evaluation, the American Air Technical Intelligence unit just as quickly discovered the maintenance problems that went along with Hien operation. In subsequent reports on tested models of the Ki.-61-Ib it was noted that the "Tony" was a pleasant aircraft to fly, but that "a great deal of maintenance was required during the trials [and] it seems likely that the Japanese find it difficult to keep the 'Tony' in commission".

The losses in New Guinea were staggering, and the J.A.A.F. never again recovered. It was as if the battle for the air over Tokyo was won over the jungle, for the J.A.A.F. loss in skilled pilots and potential instructors, plus the removal of a whole generation of mechanics and ground crewmen, left the Army air forces all but impotent. On the alert night and day, many of the Hien pilots were soon on drugs or alcohol to keep going. Hypoed-up during fighting, and suffering monumental depressions when down, many lost their health and more often their life. The rated complement for the Hien units was fifty-four aircraft and forty-eight pilots in each regiment, although this was rarely achieved and never maintained. The pilots were fed into Wewak and Hollandia by the hundreds, and always exceeded the number of available aircraft. Sickness and death kept their service numbers low. By the time the New Guinea fighting had ended the J.A.A.F. had lost ninety-five per cent of its skilled pilots having over 300 hours flying time. A comparatively small number of experienced Hien pilots survived New Guinea; among them Lieutenant Kuroki of the 33rd Regiment who survived the Pacific War with thirty-three victories, Warrant Officer Tokuyasu Ishizuka with twenty-three victories, Captain Kanshi Kishkawa with nineteen, and Sergeant Susumu Kajinami of the 68th Regiment who reportedly shot down eighteen Allied aircraft over New Guinea before his twenty-first birthday. Other older and more experienced pilots died in droves, including Major Takaji Kimura, one of the Ki.61's J.A.A.F. test pilots, who went to New Guinea as a Regimental Commander. Attacked by a P-38 in the Hien's upper-rear blind spot Kimura had twenty-six victories at the time of his death.

When the collapse finally came at Hollandia, Army personnel there were trapped. Those that escaped flew out in what they could, but many of the pilots, technical consultants, aircrews, engineering and maintenance personnel ran into the jungles to hide. This was a further critical loss to the J.A.A.F. when these experts were needed.

After June of 1944 no further attempt was made to place Japanese aircraft over New Guinea in strength. The battle had shifted to the Central Pacific, with the Philippines as the next obvious major target. The J.A.A.F. had lost favour and "face" in Tokyo, and an Imperial Order directly criticized the commanders of the 4th Air Army for "the destruction of Army Air Forces in New Guinea before they could engage in combat".

Almost superhuman attempts were made to keep the Hien relevant in the battles on the "Southern Front", with six different Ki.61 models eventually used there. The original Ki.61-Ia and Ib models were soon found to be undergunned, for downing large American bombers, and cannon was called for. Unable to meet immediate production demands in Japan, the Japanese Army made arrangements to purchase 20 mm. Mauser MG-151 cannon in Germany. Eight hundred of the cannon reached Japan by submarine in August 1943. The existing Ki.61-I wings were modified and strengthened to mount the large-bore ballistics. It was found that the MG-151 cannon could be squeezed in by turning them on their side and providing a protective fairing on the wing undersides for the cannon mechanism. While the new cannon modification entered the production line at Gifu in September 1943, technical teams from Kawasaki were rushed to New Guinea to make the same modifications in the field to create the cannon-armed Ki.61-Ia-Kai and Ki.61-Ib-Kai models. By June of 1944 the German cannon had been used up and 388 Hien fighters had been so equipped. The 33rd Fighter Regiment started out with Model I-Kai cannon-equipped Hien fighters when it went to New Guinea, with the 68th and 78th Regiments getting some of their existing aircraft modified at Wewak and other jungle airfields. New aircraft arrived already equipped with the cannons.

New Models and Units

The lessons of New Guinea, and the new design and performance opportunities possible with the Hien, led to a continuing series of experiments as well as a complete re-design of the basic airframe to improve the maintenance characteristics. The modifications began early in the Hien programme, with the first model built on production tooling in August 1942 differing from the prototypes and later production models in having a side-opening cockpit cover similar to that on the Bf.109E2.

The parallel Ki.61 project was larger and heavier, utilizing a Kawasaki Ha.40 engine derived from the DB.601A (Hideya Ando via Bueschel).

Assigned to the Army Air Inspection Division, the idea was rejected after the canopy collapsed during a flight trial. Test pilot Major Yoshitsugu Aramaki was pinned down in the cockpit by the wreckage and made a blind landing on instruments. It was later discovered that the Messerschmitt canopy was made of steel and not light dural as was the Hien cover.

Other experiments included the extensive modification of a Ki.61-Ia in the summer of 1943 to test a unique wing surface air evaporating cooling system, designed by Takeo Doi for the advanced Kawasaki Ki.64 fighter project. Better cooling and a reduced frontal section increased the Hien speed by 25 m.p.h., with the experimental model hitting 391 m.p.h. The testing ended at the close of the year after 35 flights had been completed. The idea was not considered for Hien use as the maintenance requirements were . very tricky, a poor consideration for an aircraft that was already mechanically troublesome.

Further modifications included the fitting of skis for use in the north at Paramushiro or northern Manchoukuo. Extensive trials of the ski-fitted Ki.61-Ib Hien were conducted in the winter of 1943-1944, but the modifications never became standard as war conditions changed too rapidly.

The greatest change came with the next production model of the Hien, for while it looked much like the earlier models it was an entirely new aircraft. The J.A.A.F's problems of repairing the Hien and keeping it in the air over New Guinea very quickly reached the contract negotiating tables at Kawasaki. The Army bitterly complained about the poor availability record of the Ki.61. Designers Doi and Owada were given the opportunity to design the fighter over again, only this time making greater allowances for difficult field maintenance conditions. The prototype was completed in January 1944 as the Ki.61-I-Kai-C, and known in Kawasaki records as the Model A. Japanese-made Ho.5 cannon of 20 mm. plus two 12.7 mm. Type 1 machine guns made the Kai-C armament similar to that of the earlier cannon-modified Ki.61-Ia and Ib models. The most obvious physical differences were the longer fuselage, enlarged stabiliser and fixed tail wheel, the latter replacing a troublesome retracting wheel on the earlier models. The major differences were internal. The control systems were simplified, number of total parts greatly reduced, and a detachable rear fuselage for ease of interior repairs replaced the solid fuselage of the first production models.

Evaluation of the Ki.61 series proceeded rapidly early in 1942 with twelve prototypes, the first one flying in December 1941 (Hideya Ando via Bueschel).

In addition to these changes the complete structure, with particular emphasis on the wings, was strengthened for greater combat loads. Wing fittings for tanks and armament were now possible to add to the options of military stores. As Ki.61-Ib-Kai production tapered off the new Ki.61-I-Kai-C took over, and by August 1944 it was the sole model in production.

The Kai-C remained in production until January 1945, including a small run of Ki.61-I-Kai-D examples. This was a similar aircraft, differing primarily in the mounting of 30 mm. Ho.105 cannon in the wings to replace the 20 mm. armament. Difficulties with the larger cannon soon phased out the Kai-D model, resulting in greater production of the definitive Kai-C than any other Hien model.

Some of the Kai-C production reached New Guinea, but most of these aircraft served in the Philippines and Japanese home island defence. The newer Hien units, such as the 17th, 18th, 19th, 26th, 53rd, 55th, 59th, 105th and 244th Fighter Regiments received them, while older units received Kai-C models as replacements. It was during this period that the 68th and 78th Regiments disappeared from J.A.A.F. records, being officially disbanded on 20 August 1944 in paper confirmation of their total destruction. But as old units were removed, many new units were formed throughout 1944 as Flight Training and Flight Drilling Companies. These units flew various Hien models to train the mass of new J.A.A.F. pilots needed for the coming air battles. In addition, Kai-C and Kai-D models were assigned to both the Akeno and Hitachi Air Training Divisions to speed up training for the units scheduled to go to the Philippines.

The Philippines build-up came rapidly, and once again the overseas 4th Air Army was the instrument. The J.A.A.F. units in Burma, Malaya, China and Manchoukuo were trimmed down to provide pilots and aircraft for Philippines defence, while new pilots and aircraft came out of Japan. By the time of the American invasion of the Philippines in October the 4th Air Army had over 400 aircraft in the theatre. But the J.A.A.F. had all but scraped the bottom of the barrel to accomplish this. By January 1945 this force was wiped out, and the J.A.A.F. had suffered another major defeat.

The new Hien units began to move south to the Philippines in September and October 1944. Their mission was to hold the line and settle the war on Philippine soil. The 17th Fighter Regiment under Major Yoshitsugu Aramaki flew south via Okinawa and Formosa, positioning itself to defend Manila, and by the middle of September found itself in action as American carrier planes began the strikes that preceded invasion. The 19th Regiment added its strength to Manila defence, engaging the F6F Hellcat fighters that appeared more frequently over Manila skies. Flying in tight formations of up to twenty-four aircraft, the Ki.61-I-Kai-C fighters of these units aggressively challenged the growing number of Allied planes that continued to show up. Then, on 20 October 1944, American landings were made at Leyte and the Philippine fat was in the fire. The veteran 33rd Hien Regiment was pulled out of Malaya and stationed at Clark Field on 22 October while the newer 18th and 55th Fighter Regiments flying the Hien were moved in to Luzon late in November to check the growing tide. By the end of November all of the pilots of the 55th Regiment had been killed over Leyte, and by the middle of December resistance over Leyte had stopped. On 22 December the concentrated American effort to reduce Clark Field was underway, with heavy bomber attacks being met by violent Japanese fighter reaction. The "Tony" became a familiar sight to a new generation of American pilots as the defence of Clark Field and the Manila area held for a matter of weeks. But once again the American ability to destroy massive numbers of aircraft on the ground to keep them from being a threat in the air turned the tide. Wide dispersal and the inability to assemble and react quickly kept the Hien resistance down, and soon Clark Field and its satellite strips were glutted with "Tony" wreckage. By January 1945 the battle was all but over, with J.A.A.F. and Imperial Navy air forces jointly scrambling out to safety if they could.

In one of the last engagements over the Philippines on 11 January two American pilots flying reconnaissance P-51 Mustangs ran across a Japanese naval G4M bomber modified as a transport escorted by twelve Army "Tony" fighters. They shot down nine of the fighters and the bomber, with American Congressional Medal of Honour winner William A. Shomo responsible for all but three of the "Tony" fighters as well as the death of the ranking naval air commander in the Philippines. Other surviving J.A.A.F. Hien pilots and ground crews were trapped, with the remnants of the 4th Air Army retreating into the hills of Luzon under the direction of their Commanding General as guerrilla forces.

As the Philippines campaign came to a close, the final battle had moved to Japan. It was to be the Hien's finest but most futile hour. The air assault on Japan had actually started in the summer of 1944, and promised to increase after the fall of Saipan. For most of the remainder of 1944 the raids were more of an annoyance than a war-ending threat but by the end of the year the loads and frequency were increasing. Japan had been apportioned into three areas of defence responsibility under the 6th Air Army as the Eastern, Middle and Western Defence Sectors with Hien fighters serving in all sectors. The Ki.61 became a symbol of Japan's defence, appearing on a Japanese postage stamp in the spring of 1945, particularly due to its foremost use as the defender of the Metropolitan Tokyo area under the 10th Air Division. The crack 244th Fighter Regiment under Major Teruhiko Kobayashi became the most widely publicised unit in the J.A.A.F. as the news of mainland bombings took over the front pages. The Eastern Defence Sector, which included the Yokohama-Tokyo-Nagoya complex, was ultimately protected by the Hien-equipped 18th, 23rd, 28th, 53rd and 244th Regiments. In the Middle Sector the 17th, revitalised 55th and 56th Regiments of the 11th Air Division held sway, while the 56th was ultimately transferred to the Western Sector to join the 59th Regiment of the 12th Air Division. These units had a variety of Hien models, reaching from the original Ki.61-Ia to the Kai-D. Various armament variations were also applied, with 244th Regiment Hiens stripped of their machine guns to be able to reach the B-29 above 20,000 feet. Other units added or replaced existing cannon with the 20 mm. Ho.5, the latter often protruding from the wing leading edges.

A profusion of other units were added to the air defence mix, with the Hien serving in dual training and interception roles with the 8th, and 39th Flight Training Companies, the 5th, 7th, 11th and 18th Flight Drilling Companies, and the flying schools at Akeno and Hitachi. "Tony" also became the leading Army fighter in the defence of Okinawa in April 1945 when invading Allied forces were met by Hiens of the 19th, 59th, 65th and 105th Regiments there, plus the fighters of the 23rd Independent and 37th Flight Training Companies.

The J.A.A.F. was thrust into the responsibility of protecting Japan's cities against the Boeing B-29 "Super Fortress" at a disadvantage. The operating altitude of the B-29 was well above the service ceiling of any fighter in Japanese service. "Tony" was the only single-seat fighter that could make it, but even this required stripping most of the armament off of the fighter. This put the Hien pilot at the further disadvantage of tackling an abundantly armed bomber with a totally underarmed fighter, a situation often faced by the pilots of the 244th Regiment over Tokyo. With many of the pilots fresh out of flight schools, from which pilots graduated with barely a few hours of combat flight training (a measure forced by Japan's extreme fuel shortage), the defending forces were largely weak and unskilled.

There were exceptions to this general rule. In the Eastern Defence Sector Major Teruhiko Kobayashi's 244th Regiment had an aggressive group of pilots that seasoned rapidly against the B-29. Kobayashi survived the war with twenty kills, with over ten of the B-29's. Attacking in groups of five or six from the upper front, or in a daring head-on approach, the "Tony" fighters of the 244th over Tokyo were respected by American B-29 crews. In the Middle Defence Sector the 17th Regiment was led by experienced Major Yoshitsugu Aramaki, the skilled pilot that had blind-landed the experimental Hien with the side-opening cockpit almost three years earlier. Then in the Western Defence Sector Lieut.-Colonel Furukawa led the 56th Regiment, one of the few units to receive the Model 2 Hien which was produced in limited numbers. Hien "Aces" that ran up their scores over the Home Islands included Warrant Officer Tokuyasu Ishizuka, a Ki.27-flying veteran of the pre-Pacific War fighting at Nomonhan, who downed four B-29's with his Hien, ending the war with twenty-three kills; Kanshi Ishikawa, who reportedly flew the Hien, with a total of 19 kills; and others. Hien unit commanders who gained fame over Japan included tough-minded Major Masato Kodama whose 53rd "Kodama Regiment" in the Eastern Defence Sector was regarded as one of the most disciplined units in the J.A.A.F.; Major Takefumi Kododa leading the 18th Regiment, also in the Eastern Defence Sector; Major Takahashi of the 55th Regiment in the Middle Defence Sector, whose unit was rebuilt in January 1945 and assigned to northern Kyushu defence; and Major Yoshido Takata, last commander of the 17th Regiment in the Middle Defence Sector.

The Coming of *Kamikaze*

The reality of B-29 inaccessibility and the futility of attack with light armament continually frustrated the Hien pilots over Japan. When the stories of *Kamikaze* suicide attacks by naval and ultimately by Army pilots in the Philippines captured the news media, the Army pilots defending the Japanese cities looked on this tactic as a viable way to break the grip of the B-29. Ramming became an acceptable subject for discussion, particularly since the Hien was roomy enough to let a pilot get out without difficulty. The rationale was simple. Ramming wasn't considered suicide, as the pilot had a better than even chance to survive provided the guns of the B-29 didn't get him on the final run. It was merely a way of continuing the attack once your ammunition was spent. So it began.

The acceptance of ramming as an attack form wasn't new to the Japanese. The Russians had long followed the practice; and even the British, Germans and Americans had tried it on a sporadic basis during periods of desperation. But the Japanese brought in a new element. The degree of pilot safety was negligible, and the accord offered ramming was really an emotional cop-out to allow the pilots to die for their country with honour. When the *Shinten-Seiku-Tai* "Shuddering Sky" Air Superiority Unit was formed the pilots knew their *Taiatari* "body crashing" attacks were suicidal. Yet they volunteered for the unit and prepared for the missions in training sessions that quietly and objectively told them where to smash their aircraft for the most telling effect in a B-29. Miraculously, some Hien pilots survived the experience to tell about it and inspire future neophyte *Taiatari* attackers. When Lieutenant Shinomiya rammed a B-29 in November 1944 by smashing into its vulnerable tail section with his port wing, and successfully landed his Hien after the encounter, he was a new J.A.A.F. hero. His damaged and bullet-ridden Ki.61-I-Kai-C was put on display on the ground floor rotunda of the Matsuya Department Store in the Ginza section of Tokyo over the Christmas holidays. Gusty Major Kobayashi of the 244th Regiment had two B-29 ramming kills among his score, and one *Shinten-Seiku-Tai* pilot named Nakamura survived the war with two ramming kills to his credit.

Most of the *Taiatari* pilots were killed outright, with a moment of glory on the front pages of the daily newspaper their only epitaph. The helplessness of the J.A.A.F. against the growing armada of American airpower made aerial suicide one way out of the misery of daily impotence. When Lieutenant Minoru Shirota wrote about his feelings of patriotism and then rammed a B-29 with his Hien over Nagoya on 4 January 1945 in full view of the press, the pattern was set for a rush of ramming attacks beyond that yet seen. With all armament stripped off, pilots of the "Shuddering Sky" unit took off with

nothing else in mind but smashing their Hein fighters into the vital parts of a B-29. By the end of January B-29 crews returning from Japan reported a decided increase in ramming. In one raid on urban Tokyo on 27 January some 984 fighter attacks were reported, including many ramming attempts. Five of the B-29s were downed over the target, although the B-29 crews reported the downing of sixty enemy fighters, plus seventeen probables and thirty damaged. Many of the *Taiatari* aircraft were uniquely marked, with one Hien reportedly painted all black with attacking white eagles in place of the normal *Hinomaru* insignia. Others were just as gaudy.

As the war droned on and the threat of invasion of Japan increased, Special Attack became a normal way of resistance. Pilots who volunteered were transferred from the Defence Sectors over Japan to Special Attack Corps training in which Hien fighters were equipped with 550 lb. bombs to attack invading surface units at sea. Pilots were briefly trained in navigation for the missions. Other complete units, such as the 105 Regiment on Formosa, were converted to Special Attack early in 1945. On its first sortie on 1 April 1945 the 105th could not find its targets due to weather, allowing its unarmed Hiens to return to base. They had been equipped with two 550 lb. bombs each, or a bomb load of the Hien of over 1,000 lb.

Enter the "Super Swallow"

Long before the war had entered its final phases over Japan work had progressed on improvements in the basic Hien design. Intended as Takeo Doi's masterpiece, the Model 2 re-design of the Hien would prove the superiority of Japanese engineering and establish the inline-engine fighter as the ultimate type of aircraft in its class.

As the Germans improved their standard inline fighter series with the Bf.109F, Takeo Doi and Shin Owada raced them with a larger and heavier Hien under development in 1942 and 1943 as the Ki.61-II Army Experimental Fighter. To power the new aircraft, the Ha.40 engine had been re-designed as the Ha.140 and boosted to 1,500 h.p., theoretically giving Japan a great improvement over the earlier German DB.601A design. In September 1942 the new "Super Swallow" was ready for project approval. By March 1943 the design was complete. With a larger wing to increase manoeuvrability, more power, enlarged and strengthened body and tail, the Ki.61-II was expected to achieve 400 m.p.h. But when the first aircraft was finished in August 1944, mechanical problems began to show up. By the time usable Ha.140 engines had been delivered and the Ki.61-II was ready for its flight trials in December the project was a shambles. The engine was erratic, the fuselage was unable to hold the power, and the wings cracked in flight. The project was stopped right where it was in January 1944 after the eighth prototype had been completed. The basic Hien design had been "stretched" too far and couldn't take it. Terribly depressed by the experience, both Doi and Owada struggled with their minds to determine where they had gone wrong. They then decided to utilize the new fuselage after further re-design, and go back to the proven wing of the Model I Hien. The first Ki.61-II-Kai was finished in April, and although it couldn't reach the hoped-for speed it performed better at high altitudes than any other J.A.A.F. fighter. Three more prototypes were built as the new fighter received Army approval as the Type 3 Fighter, Model 2. By September 1944 an additional twenty-six pre-production models had been completed and the way was paved to have the Model 2 Hien replace the current Ki.61-I-Kai-C on the main production lines. Just when things began to look bright again, the Hien's greatest troubles began. It wasn't until the closing weeks of the war that they were partially solved, but by then it was too late.

When production got underway on the Ki.61-II-Kai-A Model 2A Hien in October the Kagamigahara plant was immediately faced with delays with the Ha.140 engine. Almost 200 of the earlier Ki.61-I-Kai-C Hiens were already standing in the yards of the plant awaiting Ha.40

Above: Type 3, Model 1a Fighters of the 78th Air Combat Regiment caught on the ground at Wewak, northern New Guinea, summer 1943 (USAF via Bueschel).

Left: First prize! Kawasaki Hien is found at airstrip No. 2 at Cape Gloucester, New Britain, in December 1943 (Sekai no Kokuki via Bueschel).

Right: Model was Ki.61-Ia with racks under wings for bombs and tanks (USAF via Bueschel).

Above: Red tail marking identifies 2nd company. White band marking indicates company commander. Unit is 68th Air Combat Regiment (Acme via Bueschel).

Left: The Cape Gloucester Hien remained on the island for study and test into spring 1944 (USAF via Bueschel).

Right: In the air the Ki.61-Ia had a distinctive "sit" that looked like no other Japanese fighter (USAF via Bueschel).

Right: 78th Regiment Ki.61-Ia Hien in Wewak area in summer 1943. Unit was virtually annihilated there (M. Toda via Bueschel).

power plants. Engine production had been cut down to a trickle, and bombings further aggravated the situation. With the Ha.40 already in short supply, production of the bug-ridden Ha.140 was all but impossible. All that could be done was produce the Model 2A airframes as rapidly as possible, finish up those for which engines became available, and store the others as safely as possible. By the end of December over 200 were stored in sight of B-29 reconnaissance planes, along with 146 Kai-C models. By January there were 230. Ultimately only sixty-nine of the Model 2 Hiens were completed, with the other "headless" airframes standing uselessly in the plant yard and surrounding woods at a time when the J.A.A.F. was in desperate need of aircraft. Of a total production of 374, about thirty were destroyed in air raids and 275 never received their Ha.140 engines. The sixty or more Model 2 Hiens that were delivered to the J.A.A.F. entered service early in 1945. The prime production model was the 2A armed with two 12.7 mm. Type 1 machine guns and two 20 mm. Ho.5 cannon. An estimated thirty examples of the Model 2B, armed with four of the 20 mm. cannon, were included in this number. Both aircraft were equipped to carry two 550 lb. bombs and other stores. For the first time the J.A.A.F. had a fighter that could fly in formation at over 30,000 feet to challenge the B-29. With its larger canopy and greater power the Model 2 Hien was a decided improvement over the earlier models and well liked by its pilots. But the lack of engine reliability and the frequent breakdowns of the electrical system were constant sore points. Examples were delivered to the 18th, 55th, 56th and 244th Regiments, with the 56th receiving its first models on 4 May 1945. Later Model 2B examples went to these units, with deliveries also being made to the 17th, 19th and 59th Regiments and *Taiatari* units, the latter stripping the armament for air-to-air ramming.

The introduction of the Model 2 Hien coincided with a radical new development in the air battles over Japan —the arrival of Allied fighters. American carrier planes, followed by U.S.A.A.F. P-51D Mustang fighters virtually at the limit of their range from newly captured Iwo Jima, began to show up over Japan in February 1945. As the ring of Allied victories tightened on Japan, and once Okinawa had been secured, their numbers geometrically jumped. By July a British carrier force had joined the American units, and the appearance of fast fighters and bombers over Japanese cities was almost a daily occurrence. The skies over Japan became a fighter free-for-all if and when the Japanese pilots were willing to engage their enemy. The new fighter phase of Allied attack also heralded a drastic drop in Japanese opposition. With less than 200 Army aircraft defending the Tokyo area, the J.A.A.F. couldn't handle the fighter horde. Plane by plane its defensive strength was being sapped. Both sea and air cradling Japan were no longer Japanese.

Ki.100: The Desperation Fighter

The obvious mechanical and critical delivery problems of the Ha.40 and Ha.140 inline engines makes one wonder why the Kawasaki firm continued to depend on its use. Designer Doi, in a post-war interview, admitted that it would have been wise to drop the touchy power plants long before they were forced to do so. Kawasaki was quite willing to make other design adjustments, such as the development of wooden assemblies produced by outside suppliers. One such example was a plywood tail assembly that would have replaced the metal tail on the Kai-C model, with subsequent assembly as the Kai-E model, although the idea never reached production. But when it came to a basic change in power plants, Kawasaki remained inflexible. The reason was obvious, for the power plants were also produced by Kawasaki, keeping the entire production control of the Hien in the hands of the firm.

The Japanese Army's disenchantment with the producer grew rapidly as the engineless Kai-C and Model 2 airframes piled up in the Gifu area. While Kawasaki stalled and continued to work on developments of the Model 2 design, Army Air Headquarters in Tokyo began to formulate its own ideas about the future of the Hien series. Kawasaki's direction was to upgrade the Model 2 to world standards by the fitting of a bubble cockpit on the Ki.61-II-Kai-C, slated for production as the Ki.61-III Type 3 fighter, Model 3. A few examples were completed as part of the delivered Model 2's, with combat evaluation of the new variant by the 56th Regiment in the Osaka-Kobe area. On 24 October 1944, the J.A.A.F. laid down the law to the Kawasaki firm in a meeting that gave the executive group of the company little to say. In no uncertain terms the Army told the assembled group that it would tolerate no more delays. Kawasaki was informed that it would adopt the existing Model 2 airframes to the new and reliable radial Mitsubishi Ha.112-II Kinsei engine of 1,500 h.p. which was becoming available in some numbers. Army Air Headquarters assigned the Ki.100 designation to the makeshift project and demanded fast action.

The design problems seemed insurmountable. The radial engine was almost twice as wide as the existing Hien fuselage, and an entirely new mounting was required. In a crash design programme, in which a German Focke-Wulf Fw.190 A-5 fighter originally sent

SPECIFICATION—KAWASAKI Ki.61/Ki.100 HIEN

Model and Specs.	Ki.60 Prototype	Ki.60 Prototypes*	Ki.61 Prototypes	Ki.61-Kai Prototype	Ki.61-Ia	Ki.61-Ia-Kai Prototype	Ki.61-Ib	Ki.61-Ia-Kai	Ki.61-Ib-Kai	Ki.61-I-Kai-C (Ki.61-Ic)	Ki.61-I-Kai-D (Ki.61-Id)
Span (M)	9·78	10·50	12·00	12·00	12·00	12·00	12·00	12·00	12·00	12·00	12.00
Length (M)	8·40	8·47	8·75	8·75	8·75	8·75	8·75	8·75	8·75	8·94	8.94
Height (M)	2·75	3·70	3·70	3·70	3·70	3·70	3·70	3·70	3·70	3·70	3·70
Wing Area (M²)	15·90	16·20	20·00	20·00	20·00	20·00	20·00	20·00	20·00	20·00	20·00
Weight Empty (kg)	2,150	2,150	2,238	—	2,210	—	2,210	2,380	2,380	2,630	—
Weight Loaded (kg)	2,750	2,750	2,950	—	2,950	—	3,130	—	3,250	3,470	—
Weight Loaded Max. (kg)	—	—	—	—	3,250	—	3,616	—	—	—	—
Max. Speed (km/hr)	550	560/4500m	591/6,000m	—	590/5,000m	630	592/4,860m	580/5,000m	580/5,000m	560/5,000m	560/5,000m
Cruising Speed (km/hr)	—	—	—	—	—	—	400/4,000m	—	—	—	—
Climb (m/min.)	—	5,000/8'0"	—	—	—	—	5,000/5'31"	—	—	5,000/7'0"	—
Armament—M.G. (mm)	2 x 7·7 2 x 12·7	2 x 12·7	2 x 7·7 2 x 12·7**	4 x 12·7	2 x 7·7 2 x 12·7	—	4 x 12·7	2 x 7·7	2 x 12·7	2 x 12·7	2 x 12·7
Armament—Cannon (mm)		2 x 20						2 x 20	2 x 20	2 x 20	2 x 30
Armament—Bombs (kg)										2 x 250	2 x 250
Power Unit—Mfr.	Daimler-Benz	Daimler-Benz	Kawasaki	Kawasaki	Kawasaki	Kawasaki	Kawasaki	Kawasaki	Kawasaki	Kawasaki	Kawasaki
Type	DB.601A	DB.601A	Ha.40	Ha.40	Ha.40	Ha.40	Ha.40	Ha.40	Ha.40	Ha.40	Ha.40
H.P.	1,000	1,000	1,100	1,100	1,100	1,000	1,100	1,100	1,100	1,100	1,100
Crew	1	1	1	1	1	1	1	1	1	1	1
Aircraft—Mfr.	Kawasaki	Kawasaki	Kawasaki	Kawasaki	Kawasaki	Kawasaki	Kawasaki	Kawasaki	Kawasaki	Kawasaki	Kawasaki
First Built	March 1941	Summer 1941	Dec. 1941	Aug. 1942	Aug. 1942	—	Aug. 1942	Aug. 1943	Aug. 1943	Jan. 1944	Summer 1944
Number Built	1	2	12	1***	1,380‡‡	(1)‡	1,380‡‡	388‡‡‡	388‡‡‡	1,274*	1,274*

NOTE: All dimensions in original Japanese metric. Dimensions and climb in metres (m), weights in kilograms (kg), distances in kilometres (km) and speeds in kilometres per hour (km/hr.). Data in parentheses are estimates or approximate.

*Prototypes Ki.6002 and Ki.6003
**Later models had 4 x 12·7mm
***Prototype Ki.6113 with side-opening canopy

to Japan late in 1943 was dismantled to study its engine mounting dynamics, the conversion was engineered in time to have the first prototype completed in less than ninety days. The Focke-Wulf fuselage was almost as narrow as the Hien's. and the flush side mounting of the German B.M.W. 801D engine's exhausts were adopted for the Hien conversion. On 1 February 1945 the first flight of the most rapidly conceived new fighter developed in wartime Japan took place as the Ki.100 went through its paces. Two more prototypes were completed in February and March with testing progressing so satisfactorily that the new fighter was immediately adopted for service delivery as the Type 5 fighter. The all but total destruction of the Akashi engine plant by a B-29 raid in January made the new Hien adaption the only solution to continued Kawasaki fighter production, suddenly ending the use of the inline engine for fighter aircraft in Japan. Once the deadlock had been broken with acceptance as the Type 5 fighter, the conversion of existing airframes moved rapidly. By the end of March over thirty of the new fighters had been completed as the Ki.100-Ia Model 1A with the faired cockpit and armament of the original Ki.61-II-Kai-A Model 2A. By the end of May the existing airframes had been used up and the Type 5 fighter continued in original production as the Ki.100-Ib Model 1B with the bubble cockpit of the last Ki.61 Hien model. Out of the Ki.61 assemblies 272 of the Model IA were created, while an additional 118 Model 1B examples were produced before the war abruptly ended in the middle of August.

The J.A.A.F.'s new fighter proved to be a substantial improvement over the Hien model it replaced. Although the top speed of the Ki.100-Ia was slightly lower than the Ki.61-II-Kai-A with about the same rated h.p., the Type 5 fighter weighed considerably less. This difference led to a higher climb rate and a tremendous increase in manoeuvrability at altitudes at which the earlier Hien reacted sluggishly. By late March the Ki.100-Ia was being used for conversion training at the Akeno Air Training Division, with later training at Hitachi. Fighter regiments were rotated through the schools, with the 5th, 59th, 200th and 244th Regiments, plus the 81st Independent Fighter Company, receiving the Model 1A beginning in April. By May and up to the end of July, with the advent of the Model 1B, the 17th, 18th, 25th, 111th and 112th Regiments were added to the roster of units that received the Type 5 fighter. The Type 5 arrived at a time that it was desperately needed. In spite of a loss in pilot visibility and a decrease in tail efficiency due to the large radial engine, flight characteristics were most acceptable. The well-organized Hien cockpit and the ease of handling in flight made the Type 5 a perfect mount for the new pilots then being trained in J.A.A.F. flight schools with a minimum of flying time. The first use of the new fighter was against raiding B-29s, by now devastating Japan with low-altitude fire bomb raids on the cities and high-explosive raids on the aircraft industries from high altitudes. The Type 5's best altitude was approximately 20,000 feet for it was here that the aircraft was most manoeuvrable. This dropped off rapidly as the Type 5 went higher, until at 33,000 feet the fighter was almost useless. Some units, such as the 111th Regiment defending Osaka, removed the 12.7 mm. machine guns to increase the high altitude performance.

Skilled Type 5 fighter pilots were fond of the aircraft, while the younger pilots were thankful they had an aircraft they could manage so well. In spite of this, the "green" pilots were shot down almost as soon as they entered combat. Lack of skills and the tendency to stray from formation in combat cost their numbers dearly. Of the 150 or so Type 5 fighters assigned to the 111th Regiment, almost half were uselessly lost due to the inexperience of their pilots.

The most experienced and quick-to-learn pilots did far better, for in their hands the Type 5 had the edge on the F6F Hellcat and was an even match for the P-51D Mustang. Top fighter pilots had been pulled back from throughout the Empire to help in the defence of the Home Islands. Captain Hidea Inayama, a Ki.44 Shoki pilot who had flown in the defence of Palembang in the occupied Dutch East Indies, was converted to the Ki.100 and became a Company Commander in the 111th Regiment. He ended the war with twenty-two kills. Lieutenant Morikichi Kanae, a Nomonhan and Burma veteran who survived the war with thirty-two kills; and Sergeant-Major Goro Miyamoto, also a Burma veteran who survived the war with twenty-six kills, both became Ki.100 pilots with the 25th Regiment. Captain Akira Onozaki, flying the Ki.100 as a Company Commander in the 59th Regiment, ran up a tally of twenty-eight kills in New Guinea and over Japan before the war ended.

The pilots of the 111th Regiment learned to come in on the B-29s at high altitudes one at a time in head-on attacks. The skilled pilots altered their course before they came in on the final assault. Unsure pilots held their course steady as they attacked, and died as a result when the guns of the bomber calculated the approach and hit home. In fighter-to-fighter combat the advantage lay with the strong and skilled. In one crunching mêlée on 18 July 1945 a total of 25 Ki.100 fighters of

Ki.61-II Prototypes	Ki.61-II-Kai Prototypes	Ki.61-II-Kai	Ki.61-II-Kai-A (Ki.61-IIa)	Ki.61-II-Kai-B (Ki.61-IIb)	Ki.61-II-Kai (Ki.61-III)	Ki.100 Prototypes	Ki.100-Ia	Ki.100-Ib	Ki.100-II Prototypes	Ki.100-IIa	(Ki.100-IIb)
12·00	12·00	12·00	12·00	12·00	12·00	12·00	12·00	12·00	12·00	12·00	12·00
9·16	9·16	9·16	9·16	9·16	9·16	8·82	8·82	8·82	8·82	8·82	8·82
3·75	3·70	3·70	3·70	3·70	3·70	3·75	3·75	3·75	3·75	3·75	3·75
22·00	20·00	20·00	20·00	20·00	20·00	20·00	20·00	20·00	20·00	20·00	20·00
2,840	2,855	2,840	2,840	2,855	—	2,525	2,525	2,525	2,700	—	—
3,780	3,825	3,780	3,780	3,825	—	3,495	3,495	3,495	3,670	—	—
—	—	3,825	3,825	—	—	—	—	—	—	—	—
—	610/6,000m	610/6,000m	610/6,000m	600/6,000m	—	587/6,000m	—	580/6,000m	590/10,000m	—	—
—	—	—	—	—	—	—	—	400/4,000m	400/4,000m	—	—
—	5,000/6'0"	5,000/5'0"	5,000/6'0"	5,000/6'30"	—	—	—	—	5.000/6'0"	5.000/6'42"	—
2 x 12·7	2 x 12·7	2 x 12·7	2 x 12·7	—	2 x 12·7	2 x 12·7	2 x 12·7	2 x 12·7	2 x 12·7	2 x 12·7	2 x 12·7
2 x 20	2 x 20	2 x 20	2 x 20	4 x 20	2 x 20	2 x 20	2 x 20	2 x 20	2 x 20	2 x 20	2 x 20
2 x 250	2 x 250	2 x 250	2 x 250	2 x 250	2 x 250	2 x 250	2 x 250	2 x 250	2 x 250	2 x 250	2 x 250
Kawasaki	Kawasaki	Kawasaki	Kawasaki	Kawasaki	Kawasaki	Mitsubishi	Mitsubishi	Mitsubishi	Mitsubishi	Mitsubishi	Mitsubishi
Ha.140	Ha.140	Ha.140	Ha.140	Ha.140	Ha.140	Ha.112-II	Ha.112-II	Ha.112-II	Ha.112-IIru	Ha.112-IIru	Ha.112-IIru
1,500	1,500	1,500	1,500	1,500	1,500	1,500	1,500	1,500	1,500	1,500	1,500
1	1	1	1	1	1	1	1	1	1	1	1
Kawasaki	Kawasaki	Kawasaki	Kawasaki	Kawasaki	Kawasaki	Kawasaki	Kawasaki	Kawasaki	Kawasaki	Kawasaki	Nakajima
Aug. 1943	April 1944	June 1944	Aug. 1944	Sept. 1944	May 1945	1 Feb. 1945	March 1945	May 1945	May 1945	Sept. 1945§	Sept. 1945§
8	4	26**	69***	30***	(4)	3	272	118	3	None	None

‡Conversion of existing Ki.61-Ia to test wing radiators for Ki.64
‡‡Ki.61-Ia and Ki.61-Ib totals
‡‡‡Existing Ki.61-Ia and Ki.61-Ib total airframes modified to mount German Mauser Cannon

†Ki.61-Ic and Ki.61-Id totals
††Pre-production run
†††Total Ki.61-II-Kai production 374 airframes with 275 converted to Ki.110-Ia
§Intended initial production date

the 111th Regiment tangled with a greater number of American Mustangs over Osaka. Although a number of the P-51D's were downed, only four of the Japanese fighters returned to their base south of Osaka, with Captain Inayama among them. While a few others survived by parachute, most of the pilots had been killed. In another engagement over Okinawa, as reported by Radio Tokyo, a formation of eight Ki.100 fighters shot down twenty-two Hellcats out of a large group without loss to themselves, although this report has the ring of wartime propaganda to it. Whatever the results, the Type 5 fighter performed well enough in the spring and summer of 1945 to receive a citation from the J.A.A.F. for outstanding performance in combat.

The End of It All

The bombing attacks started to take their toll on Ki.100 production by June when a combination of direct attacks on the Kagamigahara plant coupled with a plant dispersal programme cut into deliveries. For the first time in the war Kawasaki had also set up another fighter production plant at Tsuiki in Miyagi Prefecture, but production was slow to get started and only twelve Type 5 fighters were produced there between May and the end of July when production ceased due to

Above: Half of the JAAF losses in New Guinea were on the ground, a mortal blow from which the Japanese Army never recovered (USAF via Bueschel).

Above: Aircraft No. 67, thought to be 78th Regiment, takes off (Sekai no Kokuki via Bueschel).

Below: Jungle camouflage took many forms, with green paint sprayed in ripples over the natural dural widely used (Sekai no Kokuki via Bueschel).

bombing. The high-altitude threat of the B-29 had to be countered or Japan would be forced to admit total defeat in the air. With its already outstanding performance the Type 5 fighter was picked for further development in March 1945 as a high-altitude supercharged fighter with a project assignment as the Ki.100-III. By adding an Ru.102 gas turbine supercharger and the properly modified Mitsubishi Ha.112-IIru engine equipped for water-methanol injection for high speed bursts, the loaded weight of the Ki.100-II jumped by some 600 lb. Streamlining was achieved by routeing the turbine air duct to the port wing root, while the turbo-supercharger itself was tucked into the underside of the fuselage in space formerly used by the shell boxes for the fuselage machine guns. When the first prototype was flown in May it was learned that the top speed had been reduced at lower altitudes but took a great jump at about 24,000 feet, thereafter exceeding the performance of the Model 1 and hitting its peak at about 33,000 feet. Three prototypes were ultimately built, with a fourth almost finished when the war ended. Examples were tested at Fussa, with at least one assigned to the 3rd Operational Training Company at Yokota to become part of the 10th Air Division, although the Ki.100-II prototypes were never used in any attacks on American bombers.

The tests, while revealing some problems in the hand-made exhaust ducts were satisfactory and the new fighter model was accepted for production at Kawasaki as the Ki.100-IIa Type 5 fighter Model 2A. The evaluation flights had shown that the Ki.100-IIa service ceiling would be 36,000 feet, while it could reach 42,000 feet if necessary. Kawasaki production for the Model 2A was scheduled for September 1945, or once the plant could get under way again. It was planned to produce the fighter there at the rate of 120 per month. In a turnabout of procurement, something Kawasaki could never achieve while producing its inline-engine fighters, the Ki.100-II was also scheduled for production at Nakajima with model variations from Kawasaki production undefined. Also scheduled to start in September 1945, the unrealistic production goal could never get off the ground as a result of Japan's unconditional surrender in August.

Thus ended the career of Japan's first new Army fighter to enter service after Pearl Harbour. Sadly, throughout its service life the Hien series was misidentified, or never recognised at all. First thought to be a Messerschmitt in its earlier Ki.61 models, the later radial-powered Ki.100 suffered the humility of not being recognised as a distinct fighter type in the closing months of the war. It was most often reported as a Nakajima Ki.84 "Frank", or just an "unidentified Japanese radial-engined fighter". The Type 5 almost earned a unique place in history when a number of them were assembled by the 5th Regiment two days after Japan's surrender for suicidal attacks on American fleet units approaching Japan south of Ise Bay. Wiser heads at Imperial Headquarters in Tokyo killed the plan. Only a few Type 5 fighters survived the war, with four of them flown by 111th pilots to Yokosuka in November 1945 for shipment to the United States for evaluation. Others ended up in museums throughout the world. The earlier Ki.61 series fared better, with examples of the Model 1B and Kai-C series left in situ in China and the former Japanese protectorate of Manchoukuo. Picked up by the Nationalists, the Hien fighters were repainted in Chinese insignia and displayed in towns and cities as prizes of war. One even survived long enough to be taken to Taiwan. The Chinese Communists, characteristically pragmatic, picked up a number of examples in Manchuria and at Peking and immediately put them in Red Army Service. Flown by mercenary Japanese pilots, the Communist Hien fighters remained in limited use until the late 1940's when they began to be replaced by more modern captured Nationalist P-51D Mustangs and imported Russian types. The best that can be said for Kawasaki's grand experiment in the inline-engine fighter is that it ended its days fighting.

Above: Captured Ki.61-Ib under test by Technical Air Intelligence Center as T.A.I.C.–9 in Southwest Pacific Area for rapid data on Hien performance (USAF via Bueschel).

Below: Photo of test Ki.61-Ib taken in the U.S., 14 March 1945 (USN via Bueschel).

Above: Captured "Tony" repainted in U.S. for use in aircraft recognition and combat training films, June 1945 (USN via Hal Andrews via Bueschel).

Above: U.S. Navy test report noted that Ki.61-Ib cockpit was "neat and convenient" and that the aircraft was "pleasant to fly" (USN via Hal Andrews via Bueschel).

Below: Ki.61-Ib of 37th Flight Training Company, Matsuyama airfield, Formosa, one of numerous combined training and home defence units set up following the loss of New Guinea (R. M. Bueschel).

Above: Line-up of cannon-equipped Hien fighters at Akeno (Sekai no Kokuki via Bueschel).

Left: Cannon-equipped Ki.61-Ib-Kai fighters were assigned to Akeno Army Flying School early in 1944 (Sekai no Kokuki via Bueschel).

Right: The Model C Hien became the defender of cities, with the 17th and 19th regiments responsible for Manila (Asahigraph via Bueschel).

Left: The "Model A" Hien Ki.61-I-Kai-C was a rugged aircraft with maintenance problems greatly simplified (R. M. Bueschel).

Right: The Model 1-Kai-C was rushed to the Philippines in autumn 1944. These are "C's" of the 18th Fighter Regiment (R. M. Bueschel).

Above: Hien of the 3rd Company, Aircraft No. 83, 19th Fighter Regiment at Clark Field, Luzon (USAF via Bielstein via Bueschel).

Above: April 1945 line-up at Clark Field with Model 1-Kai-C Hiens of 19th Regiment (USN via Hal Andrews via Bueschel).

Above: Wreckage of 2nd Company Hien of the 19th Fighter Regiment in the Philippines (Al Schmidt via Larkins via Bueschel).

Below: Hien of the 2nd Company, 19th Fighter Regiment left at Clark Field by retreating JAAF (USAF via Bielstein via Bueschel).

Above: Misfortune follows the 19th Regiment to Okinawa. Mocel 1C Hien captured intact at Okinawa. Markings of former 53rd Fighter Regiment still visible below newer unit markings (F. C. Dickey via Bueschel).

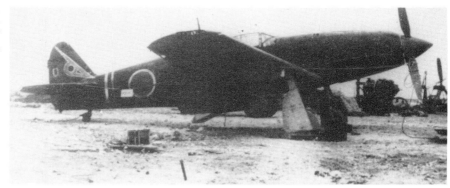

Above: Okinawa Hien carries red tail markings of the 2nd Company, 19th Regiment (R. C. Mikesh via Bueschel).

Left: Marking tapes are applied by USAF to measure dimensions to compare to existing Hien data (USAF via Bueschel).

Below: Hien losses in the Philippines created a shortage of defence fighters over Japan that was never overcome (F. C. Dickey via Bueschel).

Above: Hien fighters on dual training-defence duty at Akeno Air Training Division, late 1944 (Sekai no Kokuki via Bueschel).

Left: Ki.61-1b-Kai Mauser-cannon model at Akeno for defence fighter training in late 1944 (Sekai no Kokuki via Bueschel).

Right: Tokyo defence fighter Hien Model 1b-Kai of 244th Fighter Regiment with "White Bandage" home defence markings on wings and fuselage (Warren Shipp via Bueschel).

Left: Assigned in numbers to the newly formed Flight Training and Flight Drilling Companies in 1944, the Hien awaited the final onslaught against Japan (Asahigraph via Bueschel).

Above: Japan itself was the final front, with erratic Hien production available for defence (R. M. Bueschel).

Right: 244th Fighter Regiment had a polyglot collection of various Hien models (R. C. Mikesh via Bueschel).

Below: Line-up of 244th Fighter Regiment, Kobayashi's Hien in foreground. JAAF ''ace'' survived war with 20 victories (R. C. Mikesh via Bueschel).

Below: Later Ki.61-I-Kai-C No. 295 flown by Major Kobayashi had Headquarters Company blue markings on fuselage and wings (M. Toda via Bueschel).

Above: Regimental Commander Teruhiko Kobayashi of the 244th listed kills on side of aircraft. Hien No. 24 flown by the "ace" shows 13 victories below cockpit (M. Toda via Bueschel).

Left: 244th Regiment scrambles to defend Tokyo-Osaka area in early 1945 (M. Toda via Bueschel).

Right: Simple markings suggest Middle Defence Sector 17th Fighter Regiment (Sekai no Kokuki via Bueschel).

Right: Hien in Japan believed to be 17th or 28th Fighter Regiment (Sekai no Kokuki via Bueschel).

Left: Ki.61-I-Kai-C on home defence duty (N. Saito via Bueschel).

Above: The nose-down attitude of "Tony" was a familiar sight to American B–29 crews (Koku-Fan via Bueschel).

Above: Home defence Hien claws at sky for altitude (M. Toda via Bueschel).

Above: The Hien pilot over Japan in 1944–1945 was a "dead man". Few survived (Koku-Fan via Bueschel).

Below: Wreckage of the rammed B–29. Lieutenant Minoru Shirota became a national hero (Koku-Fan via Bueschel).

Above: An involved and relevant romantic, Shirota's articles in the aviation press thrilled thousands of Japanese readers (Koku-Fan via Bueschel).

Below: Intense national pride led to Shirota's decision to give his life for his country by the suicide ramming of a B–29 on 4 January 1945 (Koku-Fan via Bueschel).

Line-up of over twenty Model 1c Hien fighters believed to be of 26th Fighter Regiment on Formosa, late August 1945 (R. C. Mikesh via Bueschel).

A

1
Ki.61-II-Kai, 17th Air Combat Regiment, Okinawa and Formosa, June 1945.

2
Ki.61-I, 18th Air Combat Regiment, 1st Company, Philippines, November 1944.

3
Ki. 61-I-Kai, 18th Air Combat Regiment, 1st Company, Kashiwa Airfield, Chiba, Japan, June 1945.

4
Ki.61-II, 18th Air Combat Regiment, 3rd Company, Chiba, Japan 1945.

5
Ki.61-I-Kai, 18th Air Combat Regiment, 2nd Company, Chiba, Japan, August 1945.

6
Ki.61-I, 19th Air Combat Regiment, 2nd Company, Formosa, February 1944.

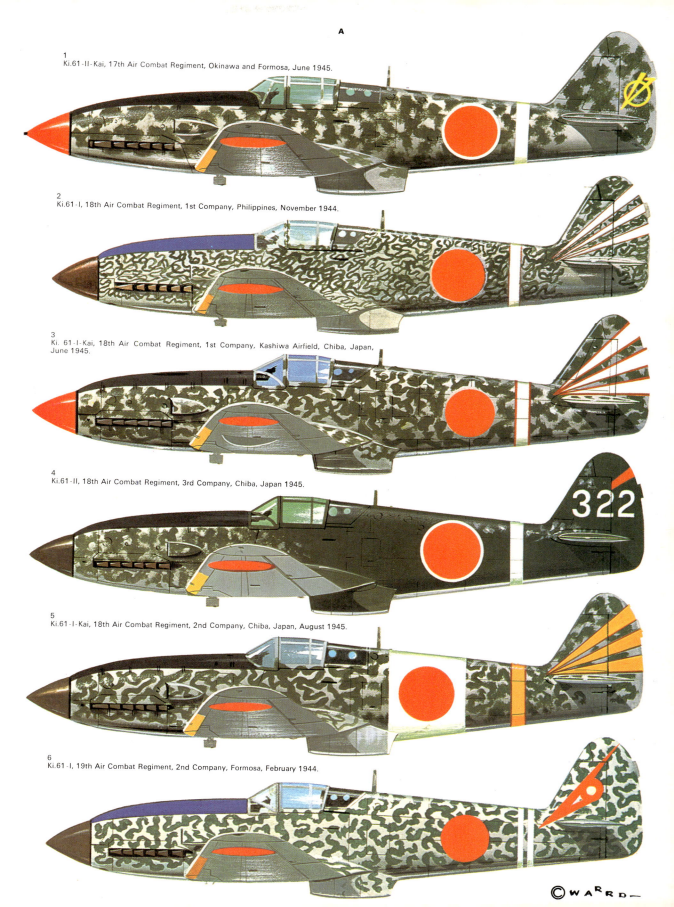

© WARD

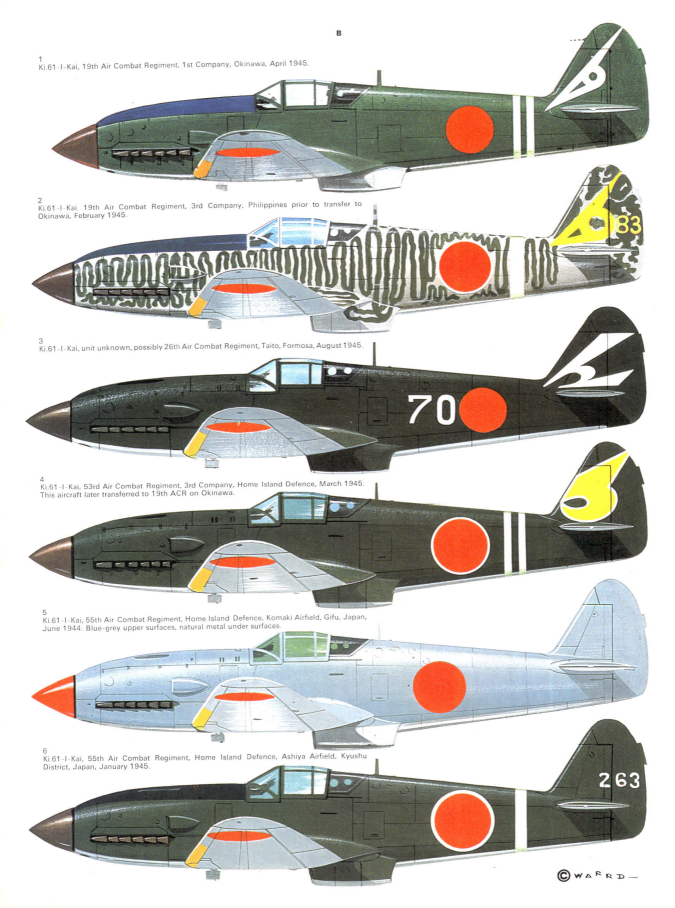

B

1
Ki.61-I-Kai, 19th Air Combat Regiment, 1st Company, Okinawa, April 1945.

2
Ki.61-I-Kai, 19th Air Combat Regiment, 3rd Company, Philippines prior to transfer to Okinawa, February 1945.

3
Ki.61-I-Kai, unit unknown, possibly 26th Air Combat Regiment, Taito, Formosa, August 1945.

4
Ki.61-I-Kai, 53rd Air Combat Regiment, 3rd Company, Home Island Defence, March 1945. This aircraft later transferred to 19th ACR on Okinawa.

5
Ki.61-I-Kai, 55th Air Combat Regiment, Home Island Defence, Komaki Airfield, Gifu, Japan, June 1944. Blue-grey upper surfaces, natural metal under surfaces.

6
Ki.61-I-Kai, 55th Air Combat Regiment, Home Island Defence, Ashiya Airfield, Kyushu District, Japan, January 1945.

© WARRD

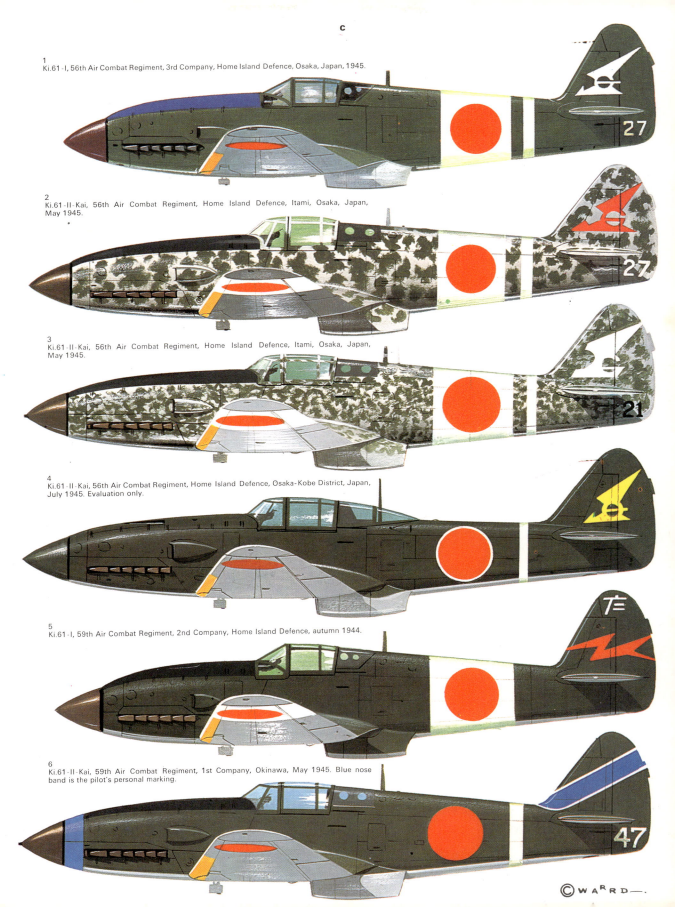

c

1
Ki.61-I, 56th Air Combat Regiment, 3rd Company, Home Island Defence, Osaka, Japan, 1945.

2
Ki.61-II-Kai, 56th Air Combat Regiment, Home Island Defence, Itami, Osaka, Japan, May 1945.

3
Ki.61-II-Kai, 56th Air Combat Regiment, Home Island Defence, Itami, Osaka, Japan, May 1945.

4
Ki.61-II-Kai, 56th Air Combat Regiment, Home Island Defence, Osaka-Kobe District, Japan, July 1945. Evaluation only.

5
Ki.61-I, 59th Air Combat Regiment, 2nd Company, Home Island Defence, autumn 1944.

6
Ki.61-II-Kai, 59th Air Combat Regiment, 1st Company, Okinawa, May 1945. Blue nose band is the pilot's personal marking.

© WARRD

D

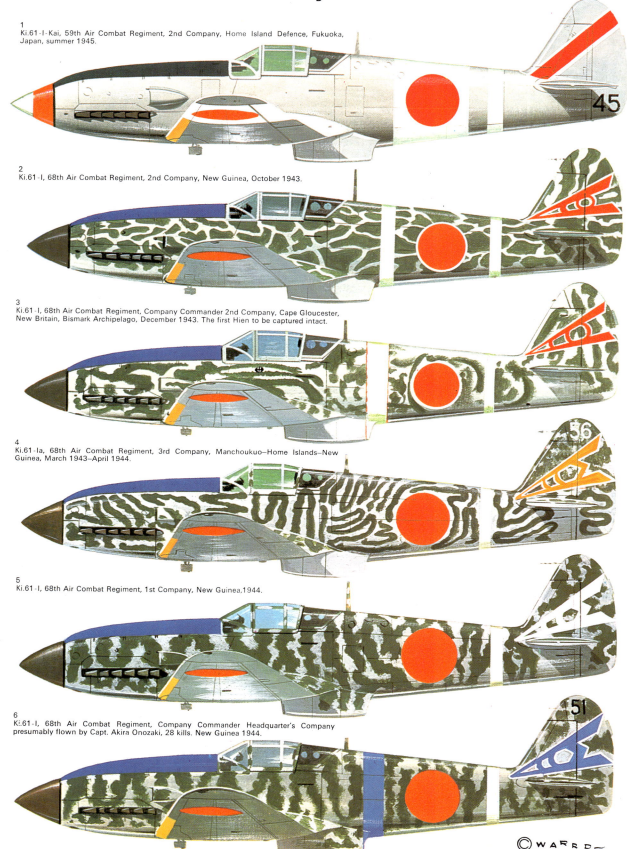

1
Ki.61-I-Kai, 59th Air Combat Regiment, 2nd Company, Home Island Defence, Fukuoka, Japan, summer 1945.

2
Ki.61-I, 68th Air Combat Regiment, 2nd Company, New Guinea, October 1943.

3
Ki.61-I, 68th Air Combat Regiment, Company Commander 2nd Company, Cape Gloucester, New Britain, Bismark Archipelago, December 1943. The first Hien to be captured intact.

4
Ki.61-Ia, 68th Air Combat Regiment, 3rd Company, Manchoukuo—Home Islands—New Guinea, March 1943—April 1944.

5
Ki.61-I, 68th Air Combat Regiment, 1st Company, New Guinea,1944.

6
Ki.61-I, 68th Air Combat Regiment, Company Commander Headquarter's Company presumably flown by Capt. Akira Onozaki, 28 kills. New Guinea 1944.

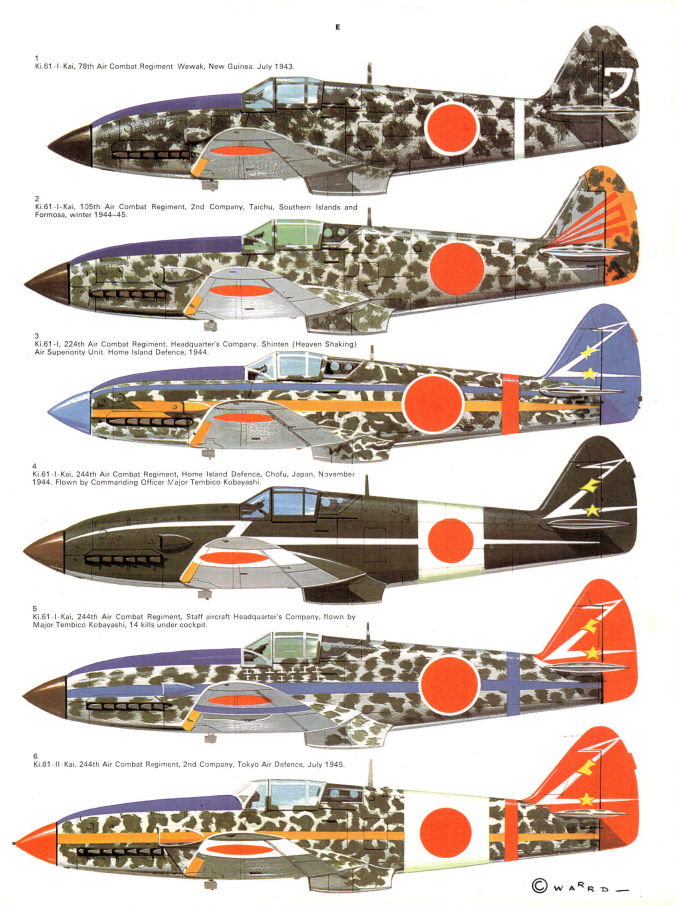

1
Ki.61-I-Kai, 78th Air Combat Regiment Wewak, New Guinea. July 1943.

2
Ki.61-I-Kai, 105th Air Combat Regiment, 2nd Company, Taichu, Southern Islands and Formosa, winter 1944–45.

3
Ki.61-I, 224th Air Combat Regiment, Headquarter's Company. Shinten (Heaven Shaking) Air Superiority Unit. Home Island Defence, 1944.

4
Ki.61-I-Kai, 244th Air Combat Regiment, Home Island Defence, Chofu, Japan, November 1944. Flown by Commanding Officer Major Tembico Kobayashi.

5
Ki.61-I-Kai, 244th Air Combat Regiment, Staff aircraft Headquarter's Company, flown by Major Tembico Kobayashi, 14 kills under cockpit.

6
Ki.61-II-Kai, 244th Air Combat Regiment, 2nd Company, Tokyo Air Defence, July 1945.

© WARD

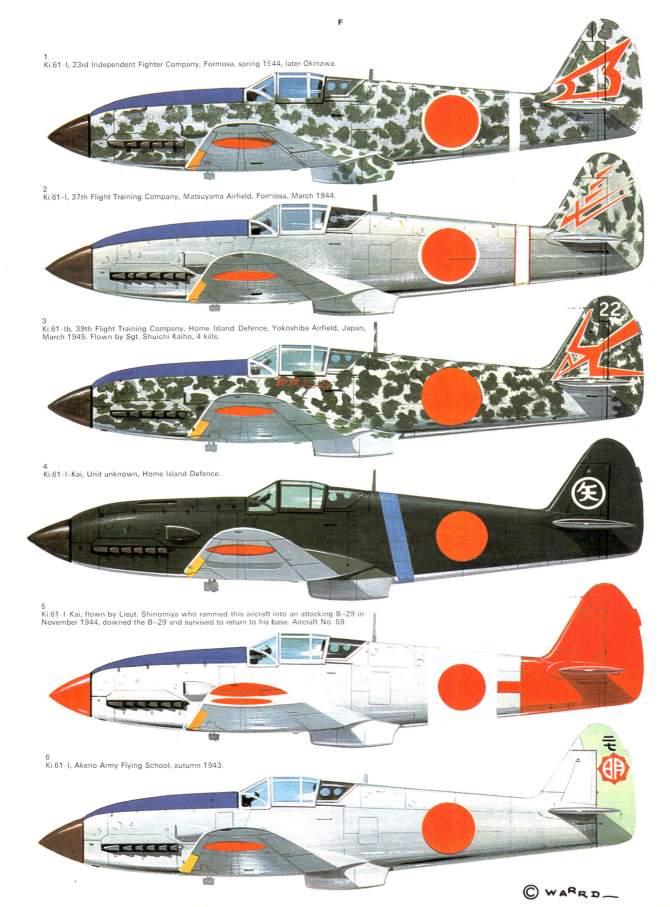

F

1
Ki.61-I, 23rd Independent Fighter Company, Formosa, spring 1944, later Okinawa.

2
Ki.61-I, 37th Flight Training Company, Matsuyama Airfield, Formosa, March 1944.

3
Ki.61-Ib, 39th Flight Training Company, Home Island Defence, Yokoshiba Airfield, Japan,
March 1945. Flown by Sgt. Shuichi Kaiho, 4 kills.

4
Ki.61-I-Kai, Unit unknown, Home Island Defence.

5
Ki.61-I-Kai, flown by Lieut. Shinomiya who rammed this aircraft into an attacking B-29 in
November 1944, downed the B-29 and survived to return to his base. Aircraft No. 59.

6
Ki.61-I, Akeno Army Flying School, autumn 1943.

© WARD

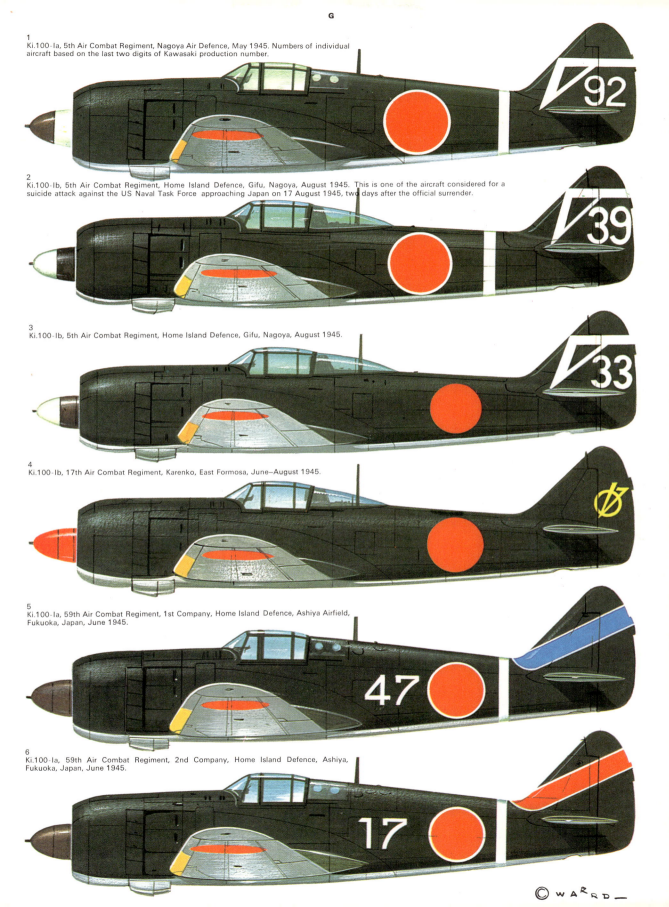

1
Ki.100-Ia, 5th Air Combat Regiment, Nagoya Air Defence, May 1945. Numbers of individual aircraft based on the last two digits of Kawasaki production number.

2
Ki.100-Ib, 5th Air Combat Regiment, Home Island Defence, Gifu, Nagoya, August 1945. This is one of the aircraft considered for a suicide attack against the US Naval Task Force approaching Japan on 17 August 1945, two days after the official surrender.

3
Ki.100-Ib, 5th Air Combat Regiment, Home Island Defence, Gifu, Nagoya, August 1945.

4
Ki.100-Ib, 17th Air Combat Regiment, Karenko, East Formosa, June–August 1945.

5
Ki.100-Ia, 59th Air Combat Regiment, 1st Company, Home Island Defence, Ashiya Airfield, Fukuoka, Japan, June 1945.

6
Ki.100-Ia, 59th Air Combat Regiment, 2nd Company, Home Island Defence, Ashiya, Fukuoka, Japan, June 1945.

1
Ki.100-Ia, 59th Air Combat Regiment, 3rd Company, Home Island Defence, Ashiya, Fukuoka, Japan, June 1945.

2
Ki.100-Ib, 111th Air Combat Regiment, 1st Company, Home Island Defence, Komaki, Gifu, Japan, August 1945.

3
Ki.100-Ib, 111th Air Combat Regiment, 2nd Company, Home Island Defence, Komaki, Gifu, Japan, August 1945.

4
Ki.100-Ia, 244th Air Combat Regiment, 1st Company, Home Island Defence, Eastern Defence Sector. April–July 1945.

5
Ki.100-Ia, 244th Air Combat Regiment, 2nd Company, Home Island Defence, Eastern Defence Sector. April–July 1945.

6
Ki.100-Ib, 244th Air Combat Regiment, 1st Company, Home Island Defence, Chofu, Tokyo, July 1945.

© WARD

Right: Ki.61-II-Kai-A as assigned to the Shinten-Seiku-Tai suicide ramming detachment of the 244th Fighter Regiment (H. McCormick via Bueschel).

Left: Ki.61-I-Kai-D in home defence markings, unit unknown (R. M. Bueschel).

Right: Model variant of Model 2 Hien produced as the Model III with bubble cockpit, shown with aircraft in markings of 56th Fighter Regiment (Sekai no Kokuki via Bueschel).

Left: When the Pacific War abruptly ended, Hien wreckage littered Japan's empire (Koku-Fan via Bueschel).

Right: The Hien was favoured as a ramming type as the pilot at least had a slight chance to get out of the roomy cockpit (Hiko Shonen via Bueschel).

Above: Hien Model 2A can be quickly identified by larger scoop, longer nose (Akira Hasegawa via Bueschel).

Left: Without question the most troublesome power plant in any Pacific War production fighter—the unreliable Kawasaki Ha.140 of 1,500 erratic h.p. (Akira Hasegawa via Bueschel).

Below: Completely redesigned, the "Tony 2" had longer fuselage, improved visibility and more powerful engine than the "Tony 1" (Akira Hasegawa via Bueschel).

Above: Early Model 1b Hien survived war in China to be recaptured a few days after this photo was taken by Chinese Communists. Shown in Nationalist insignia at Peiping on 16 November 1945 (Peter M. Bowers via Bueschel).

Below: Model 1-Kai-C Hien at Nanyuan Airfield, Peiping, in September 1945. These fighters toured the mainland as war trophies (Peter M. Bowers via Bueschel).

Above: 5 Sen of 5th Regiment is airborne (N. Saito via Bueschel).

Right: In the air the Ki.100 combined "Tony" attitude with radial engine. American B-29 crews were unable to identify it as a distinct aircraft type, confusing it with Ki.84 "Frank" (N. Saito via Bueschel).

Below: Successor to the Hien. Ki.100-Ia Type 5 Fighter mated Ki.61-IIa fuselage with Kinsei 62 radial engine (Sekai no Kokuki via Bueschel).

Below: Aircraft No. 88 of 5th Fighter Regiment, Nagoya, in May 1945, taking off on interception (N. Saito via Bueschel).

Above: Service evaluation prototype of Ki.100 Model Ib with bubble cockpit (Kawasaki via Bueschel).

Below: Type 5 Model Ia Fighters of 59th Fighter Regiment at Ashiya Airfield, Fukuoka, Japan, June 1945. Blue tail markings of 1st Company on Aircraft No. 177 (R. C. Mikesh via Bueschel).

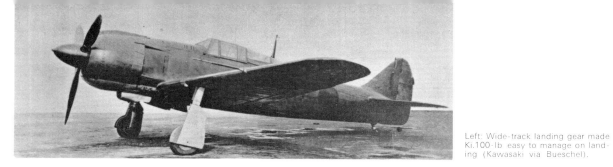

Left: Wide-track landing gear made Ki.100-lb easy to manage on landing (Kawasaki via Bueschel).

Right: Type 5 Fighter of the 111th Fighter Regiment, assigned to Middle Defence Sector protection (Sekai no Kokuki via Bueschel).

Left: The bubble cockpit of the Ki.61-III became a production feature of the Ki.100-lb (Koku-Fan via Bueschel).

Below: Service deliveries of the Model 1B began in June 1945 (M. Toda via Bueschel).

The Ki.100-Ib in operational service with the 5th Fighter Regiment, Nagoya, early August 1945 (N. Saito via Bueschel).

Above: 5th Regiment 5 Sen (Type 5 Fighter) prepares to take off (N. Saito via Bueschel).

Below: Aircraft No. 39 identification is based on last two digits of Kawasaki production number marked on data plate of aircraft (N. Saito via Bueschel).

Below: Line-up of 5th Regiment at Gifu, Nagoya in rare moment of repose, August 1945 (N. Saito via Bueschel).

Above: 5th Regiment flew Ki.100 (foreground) and Kawasaki Ki.45-kai Toryu on B–29 interception duties (N. Saito via Bueschel).

Below: Most Ki.100 pilots were "green" as many Army veterans had been killed over New Guinea or Japan (N. Saito via Bueschel).

Above: Bomb racks on outer wing panels were used for fuel, or removed to lighten weight (N. Saito via Bueschel).

Right: Simple cockpit of Ki.100-lb inherited from Ki.61 series made Type 5 Fighter a pleasure to fly (Maru via Bueschel).

Below: A number of Ki.100-lb aircraft survived the war to be demobilized. Note removal of propeller (M. B. Passingham via Bueschel).

Right : Nose-heavy attitude of Ki.100-Ib reduced tail efficiency, but problem was only minor (M. Olmsted via Bueschel).

Left: Ki.100 wreckage went unrecognized until type was identified by Japanese in interviews with American interrogators (M. Olmsted via Bueschel).

Right: Former 111th Fighter Regiment Ki.100-Ib sent to United States for evaluation (M. Olmsted via Bueschel).

Left: Under evaluation by the JAAF, the Ki.100 Model 2 was supercharged for high altitude B-29 interception (R. C. Mikesh via Bueschel).

Right: Ki.100 Model 2 was slated for mass production in 1945–1946. Markings are 3rd Operational Training Company at Yokota. Colour scheme was overall medium grey with white tail markings (R. C. Mikesh via Bueschel).

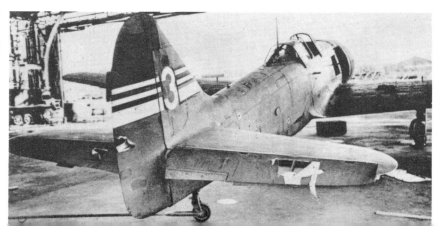

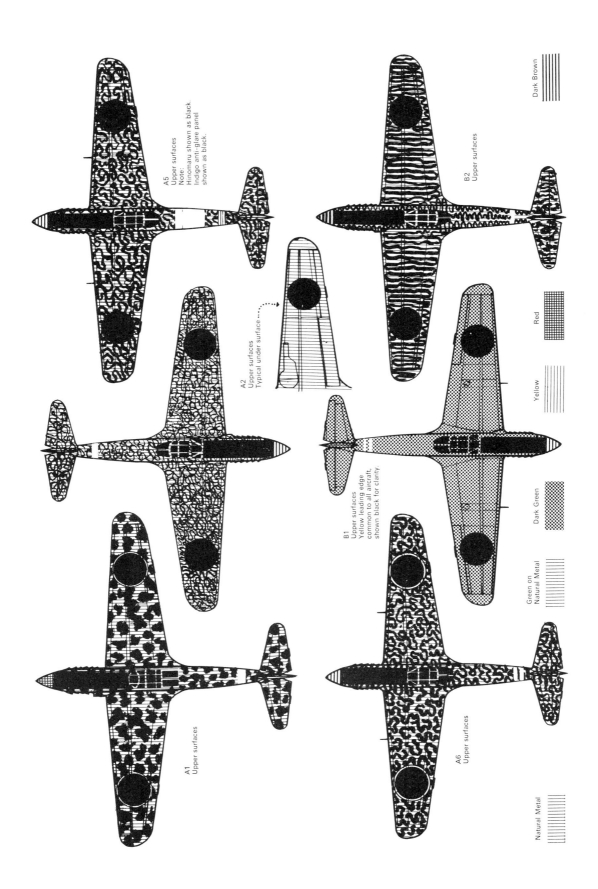

A5
Upper surfaces
Note:
Hinomaru shown as black.
Indigo anti-glare panel
shown as black.

B2
Upper surfaces

A2
Upper surfaces
Typical under surface

B1
Upper surfaces
Yellow leading edge
common to all aircraft,
shown black for clarity.

A1
Upper surfaces

A6
Upper surfaces

Dark Brown

Red

Yellow

Dark Green

Green on
Natural Metal

Natural Metal

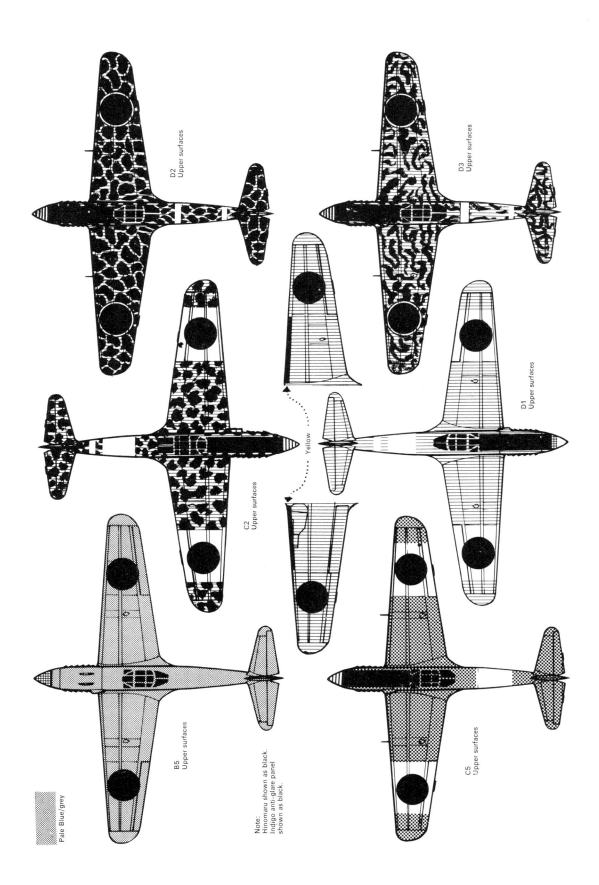

D2
Upper surfaces

D3
Upper surfaces

D1
Upper surfaces

C2
Upper surfaces

Yellow

B5
Upper surfaces

C5
Upper surfaces

Pale Blue/grey

Note:
Hinomaru shown as black.
Indigo anti-glare panel
shown as black.

G1
Upper surfaces

Note: Under surfaces

Natural Metal
A1,2,3,5,6:
B1,2,5:
C2,3:
D1,2,3,4,5,6:
E1,2,3,5,6:
F1,2,3,5,6:
G1,2,3,4,5,6:
H1,6:

Pale Grey
A4:
B3,4,6:
C1,4,5,6:
E4:
F4:

Very Pale Grey
H2,3:

Pale Grey/Green
H4,5:

H2
Upper surfaces

F5
Upper surfaces
Red shown as black
except for spinner.

F6
Upper surfaces

Chinese insignia
neatly superimposed over
Hinomaru all positions,
scheme otherwise standard JAAF

E4
Upper surfaces
Note:
Hinomaru shown as black.
Indigo anti-glare panel
shown as black.

E6
Upper surfaces

JAPANESE ARMY AIR FORCES (JAAF)
UNITS OPERATING Ki.61 TYPE 3 FIGHTER Hien

AIR COMBAT REGIMENTS:

Regiment	When used	Area of Operations	Former A/C	Later A/C	Comments
17th Fighter	10 Feb. 1944–June 1945	Japan Philippines Japan (Middle Defence Sector) Formosa	None	Ki.100	Unit formed at Kagamigahara, Gifu, Japan on 10 Feb. 1944 with Ki.61 as original equipment. Assigned to Philippines summer 1944. Manila air defence. Commander was Major Yoshitsugi Aramaki. Fought at Leyte.
18th Fighter	10 Feb. 1944–end of war	Japan Philippines Japan (Eastern Defence Sector)	Ki.27	Ki.100	Unit formed at Kashiwa, Chiba, Japan on 10 Feb. 1944 with Ki.61 as original combat equipment. Rushed to Philippines in Nov. 1944 and fought in central and south Philippines. Commander was Major Takefumi Kododa.
19th Fighter	10 Feb. 1944–end of war	Japan Philippines Formosa Okinawa	None	None	Unit formed on Formosa on 10 Feb. 1944 with Ki.61 as original equipment. Manila air defence. Pulled back to Formosa, and thrown into Okinawa April 1945. Unit disbanded at Shinchi Kushu, Formosa at end of war.
23rd Fighter	11 Oct. 1944–end of war	Japan (Eastern Defence Sector)	Ki.43 Ki.44	Ki.84	Home Island Defence unit. Ki.61 augmented Ki.43 and Ki.44. Formerly a training company at Ota Airfield. Unit disbanded at Inba, Chiba, Japan at end of war.
26th Fighter	Late 1944–end of war	Formosa	Ki.51b Ki.43	None	Decimated Ki.43 unit reformed after return from New Guinea. Rebuilt with Ki.61 as original equipment for Home Island Defence. Unit disbanded at Taito, Formosa at end of war.
28th Fighter	April 1944–July 1945	Japan (Eastern Defence Sector)	Ki.15 Ki.36 Ki.46 Ki.51	Ki.46-III-Kai Ki.102	Former Reconnaissance Company converted to Fighter. Unit pulled back from Manchoukuo. Former 28th Independent Company. Reformed in April 1944 with Ki.61 as original equipment. Disbanded at Togane, Chiba, Japan in July 1945.
33rd Fighter	Late 1943–end of war	New Guinea Philippines Manchoukuo Dutch East Indies	Ki.10 Ki.27 Ki.43	None	One of the most active JAAF units. "Ace" Lieut. Kuroki scored 33 kills and flew Ki.61 in New Guinea. Unit sent to Philippines in Sept. 1944. Pulled out for strategic defence. Ended war at Medan, Dutch East Indies.
53rd Fighter	23 March 1944–March 1945	Japan (Eastern Defence Sector)	None	Ki.45-Kai	Unit formed at Tokorozawa, Saitama, Japan for Home Island Defence on 23 March 1944. Flew Ki.61 for a short period, then converted to Ki.45-Kai for B-29 interception. Original Ki.61 aircraft reassigned to other duties.
55th Fighter	30 May 1944–end of war	Japan Philippines Japan (Middle Defence Sector)	None	None	Unit formed at Komaki, Gifu, north of Nagoya, Japan, on 30 May 1944 with Ki.61 as original equipment. Assigned to Philippines reinforcements Nov. 1944. All pilots killed at Leyte. Reformed in Japan for Home Island Defence. Commander in Philippines was Major Takahashi. Last Commander in Japan was Major Kenjiro. Unit disbanded at Sano, Nara, Japan at end of war.
56th Fighter	26 April 1944–end of war	Japan (Middle Defence Sector) Japan (Western Defence Sector)	Ki.43	None	Began flight training on Ki.61 under Lieut. Col. Furukawa in April 1944. Unit officially formed on 26 April 1944 at Taisho, Osaka, Japan. Moved to Kyushu in Aug. 1944. Ended war in defence of Osaka-Kobe district. Disbanded at Itami, Osaka at end of war.
59th Fighter	Late 1944–end of war	Japan (Western Defence Sector) Okinawa	Ki.27 Ki.43	Ki.100	Crack JAAF unit. Returned to Japan for Home Defence from overseas service. Used as day interceptor unit over Japan. Commander was Captain Akira Onozaki, an "ace" with 28 kills. Unit sent to Okinawa April 1945. Disbanded at Ashiya, Fukuoka, Japan at end of war.
65th Fighter	Summer 1944–end of war	Philippines Formosa Okinawa Japan	Ki.32 Ki.51b Ki.43	Ki.45-Kai	Replacement for Ki.43 in one of the "Old Units" of the JAAF. Unit shifted frequently as war pressed on Home Islands. Decimated at Okinawa. Final use was Home Defence in Japan. Unit disbanded at Metabaru, Saga, Japan at end of war.
68th Fighter	March 1943–April 1944	Manchoukuo New Guinea	Ki.27 Ki.43	None	First combat unit to receive Ki.61. Converted to Ki.61 from Ki.27 in March 1943 and moved to New Guinea in April 1943. Virtually annihilated in New Guinea. Also flew convoy protection out of Rabaul. Unit officially removed from records 20 Aug. 1944.
78th Fighter	April 1943–April 1944	Japan Rabaul New Britain New Guinea	Ki.27	None	Converted to Ki.61 from Ki.27 at Akeno Army Flying School in April 1943 and moved to Rabaul in May and New Guinea in June. Virtually annihilated in New Guinea, at Wewak Airfield. Unit officially removed from records at Sarumi, SE Asia, 20 Aug. 1944.
105th Fighter	August 1944–end of war	Formosa Okinawa Formosa	None	None	Home Islands Defence unit formed at Taichu, Formosa on 25 July 1944 with Ki.61 as original equipment. Moved into Okinawa for defence in spring 1945 and suffered great losses. Returned to Formosa as a Special Attack Regiment. Disbanded at Giran, Formosa at end of war.
244th Fighter	Oct. 1944–end of war	Japan (Middle Defence Sector) Japan (Eastern Defence Sector)	Ki.27	Ki.100	Former 144th Regiment reformed as 244th and re-equipped with Ki.61 in Oct. 1944 at Chofu, Tokyo. Crack Air Defence unit, Tokyo area. Commander was Major Tembico Kobayashi, an "ace" with 20 kills. Disbanded at Yokaichi, Shiga, Japan at end of war.

INDEPENDENT COMPANIES:

Company	When used	Area of Operations		Former A/C	Later A/C	Comments
15th Fighter	Oct. 1944– end of war	Japan	China	Ki.43	None	Home Island Defence unit. Picked for Special Attack duties. Both Ki.43 and Ki.61 were original equipment.
23rd Fighter	20 Jan. 1944– end of war	Japan Okinawa	Formosa	None	None	Home Island Defence unit formed in Jan. 1944 with Ki.61 as original equipment. Assigned to Formosa in spring 1944. Took part in Okinawa fighting in April 1945, including Special Attack missions.

FLIGHT TRAINING COMPANIES:

Company	When used	Area of Operations		Former A/C	Later A/C	Comments
8th	31 March 1944– 7 June 1945	Japan		None	None	One of the first Flight Training Companies. Formed 31 March 1944 with Ki.61 as original equipment. Operational training, and also utilized for interception of B-29 over Japan. Disbanded 7 July 1945
37th	21 Feb. 1944– end of war	Formosa Formosa	Okinawa	None	None	Unit formed at Taipei, Formosa in Feb. 1944 with Ki.61 as original equipment. Purpose was operational training, although doubled as Home Island Defence. Thrown into Okinawa battle. Often misidentified as 37th Regiment.
39th	31 July 1944– end of war	Japan		Ki.43 Ki.79	None	Unit stationed at Yokoshiba Airfield, Japan. Purpose was operational training, although Ki.61 doubled as B-29 interceptors in spring 1945.

FLIGHT DRILLING COMPANIES:

Company	When used	Area of Operations	Former A/C	Later A/C	Comments
5th	31 May 1944– end of war	Japan	Ki.27, Ki.36, Ki.43, Ki.51	None	Unit formed 31 May 1944 and disbanded at end of war.
7th	20 June 1944– end of war	Japan	Ki.27, Ki.36, Ki.51	None	Unit formed 20 June 1944 and disbanded at end of war.
11th	30 Nov. 1944– end of war	Japan	None	None	Formed 30 Nov. 1944 with Ki.61 as original equipment. Disbanded at end of war.
17th	3 Oct. 1944– end of war	Japan	Ki.43	None	Formed 3 Oct. 1944 with both Ki.43 and Ki.61 as original equipment. Disbanded at end of war.
18th	30 Oct. 1944– 1 Aug. 1945	Japan	None	None	Formed 30 Oct. 1944 with Ki.61 as original equipment. Disbanded two weeks before end of war on 1 Aug. 1945.

TRAINING SCHOOLS:

School	When used	Area of Operations	Former A/C	Later A/C	Comments
Akeno Army Flying School	March 1943– 20 June 1944	Akeno, Japan	Ki.10, Ki.27, Ki.43, Ki.44	Ki.45 Ki.84	Trained 68th Regiment in March and 78th Regiment in April 1943, and additional units thereafter. First school to provide Ki.61 training.
Akeno Air Training Division	20 June 1944– 10 July 1945	Akeno, Japan	Ki.43 Ki.44 Ki.45	Ki.84 Ki.100	Akeno Army Flying School reformed 20 June 1944 in JAAF reorganization. Ki.61 training was centred at Akeno. School officially terminated 10 July 1945.
Hitachi Air Training Division	20 June 1944– 10 July 1945	Hitachi, Japan	Ki.44	Ki.100	School formed on 20 June 1944 as autonomous unit for Ki.44 training, later adding Ki.61. Formerly part of Akeno Army Flying School. School officially terminated 10 July 1945.
Army Aviation Maintenance School	March 1943– June 1943	Tokorozawa, Japan	91-Sen 92-Sen Ki.10, Ki.27, Ki.43, Ki.44	Ki.45	Maintenance and repair training for 68th and 78th Regiments began in spring 1943. In June 1943 school was reformed as the Tokorozawa Army Aviation Maintenance School.
Tokorozawa Army Aviation Maintenance School	June 1943– end of war	Tokorozawa, Japan	All current JAAF aircraft	All current JAAF aircraft	Ground crew maintenance and repair training for all JAAF Regiments. Began with Ki.61. Training for Home Defence units continued throughout the war.
Tachikawa Instructing Maintenance Division	Autumn 1944– end of war	Tachikawa, Japan	All current JAAF aircraft	All current JAAF aircraft	Maintenance and repair training for Philippines, Okinawa and Home Defence units.

TAIATARI (Special Attack):

Regiment	When used	Area of Operations		Former A/C	Later A/C	Comments
105th Special Attack	April 1945– end of war	Okinawa (Southern Islands)	Formosa	None	None	Following Okinawa campaign 105th Regiment officially became a Special Attack Corps. Stationed in Southern Islands below Formosa. Surviving remnants of unit disbanded at Giran, Formosa at end of war.
244th Special Attack	May 1945– end of war	Chofu, Japan Yokaichi, Japan		None	Ki.100	Various company units of the 244th at Chofu Airfield defending Tokyo used as Air Superiority units; task was air-to-air ramming of B-29's. Unit remnants disbanded at Yokaichi, Shiga, Japan at end of war.

FOREIGN SERVICE:

Unit and Country	When used	Area of Operations		Comments
Republic of China (Nationalist China)	Aug. 1945–1947	North China	Central China	Captured in some numbers by the Nationalists in Central and North China. Temporary CAF (Chinese Air Force) unit formed with Ki.61 at Nanyuan Airfield, Peiping, Sept. 1945. Most of these aircraft lost when Communists overran Manchuria and North China.
Red Army of China (Communist China)	Oct. 1945– July 1946	Manchuria	North China	Former JAAF and CAF examples captured in Manchuria and at Peiping. Flown in Red Army Air Force service by Japanese pilots. One of first fighters available in numbers in Red Army of China service.
People's Liberation Army Air Force (Communist China)	July 1946–1949	North China	Central China	PLAAF (People's Liberation Army Air Force) formed in July 1946 with Ki.61 as one of original fighters in use. Sporadic use in Chinese Civil War, although Nakajima radial fighters Ki.43, Ki.44 and Ki.84 were favoured.